Wicklow County
County Library Services

KW-480-701

THE GREAT IRISH BANK ROBB€RY

The Inside Story of Conflict, Betrayal & Corporate Greed in Irish Banking

by
LIAM COLLINS

MENTOR
BOOKS

WICKLOW COUNTY COUNCIL

Date Recd

Accession No: 30006004088903
Price: EUR11.99
20456
IRISH LIBRARY SUPPLIERS LTD.
080401

332.10945

published in 2007 by

Mentor Books Ltd.
43 Furze Road,
...yford Industrial Estate,
Dublin 18.
Republic of Ireland

Tel. +353 1 295 2112/3   Fax. +353 1 295 2114
e-mail: admin@mentorbooks.ie
www.mentorbooks.ie

A catalogue record for this book is available
from the British Library

Copyright © Liam Collins

The right of Liam Collins to be identified as the author of this
work has been asserted by him in accordance with the Copyright,
Design and Patents Act 1988.

All rights reserved. No part of this publication may be reproduced,
stored in a retrieval system, or transmitted in any form or by any
means electronic, mechanical, photocopying, recording, or
otherwise, without prior written permission of the publisher.

ISBN: 978-1-84210-393-7

Cover by Anú Design
Editing and design by Mentor Books

Printed in Ireland by ColourBooks Ltd.

Contents

1	A Big Brown Envelope	1
2	James Livingstone Goes to Milltown Malbay	18
3	Main Street, New York	26
4	A Culture of Greed	34
5	Two Little Boys	44
6	The Dana Affair	54
7	Ireland 1991	63
8	Shafting Spollen	82
9	DIRT on the DART	88
10	Spollen Fights Back	104
11	Crisis on the Fourth Floor	122
12	The Board Decides	131
13	Sealing in the Smell	148
14	Murder in Malahide	158
15	Sunday Morning Coming Down	168
16	A Second Amnesty, Perhaps	178
17	Committee Room Deliberations	191
18	The Customer Is Always Right	204
19	Drama at the Hearings	219
20	Bringing Home the Bacon	227
21	The Result	240
22	A Red Ferrari and God's Banker	250

Foreword

It all began when Liam Collins broke a story in the *Sunday Independent* in April 1998. It was a story of massive fraud, with thousands of crooks stealing countless millions of pounds with the help of Allied Irish Banks, using bogus non-resident accounts. The media did its job. Liam's story and *Magill* the following October, brought to light a scandal the State knew had happened, but had kept from the rest of us.

It's questionable if anything would have stirred without the media revelations. The scandal led to an investigation by the Comptroller and Auditor General, which found that all the banks were at it. The setting up of the DIRT inquiry – which led to the banks having to hand over IR£173 million in ill-gotten gains plus the hundreds of millions from the tax dodgers meant that Liam Collins's revelations kicked off a process that led to the State retrieving a huge financial windfall. And in my book, that warrants a small gesture of acknowledgement. Even if only a piece of headed notepaper with the word 'thanks' scribbled on it. The kind of thing you can hang on your wall, and one day point to and tell the grandkids about it. It must be nice to be just a small but not inconsiderable part of that.

Liam Collins didn't set out to replenish the coffers of the State. He was motivated solely by that perennial journalistic Holy Grail: a good story. A good yarn. Something to make everyone sit up on Sunday and go: 'Wow.' He was just doing his job. It's just that in some areas of public life that hasn't been fashionable. If politicians were doing their job, they would have fought tax evasion with legislation, by political campaigning, and by beefing up the appropriate section of the Garda. They would have backed up the rank and file tax inspectors who, from the late 1970s were signalling that something was wrong.

Instead, they simpered over a blatantly corrupt Haughey, patted tax-dodgers on the back and panhandled business interests for the money to buy funny hats at election time.

And had the Revenue done their job, they would have confronted the lawbreakers they knew about from the 1970s when the likes of Des Traynor treated the tax inspectors like dirt.

Now, if you'll excuse me, I'll head down to the off-licence to purchase a decent bottle of wine which I will place on Mr Collins's desk. A small token, on behalf of the people of Ireland – since the State hasn't bothered to acknowledge it – of thanks to Liam for doing his job, and upholding one of journalism's noble traditions.

Gene Kerrigan

Acknowledgements

Aengus Fanning, editor of the *Sunday Independent*, who published the story.

Niall Murphy, a former employee of AIB who suggested this book a decade ago.

Pat Rabbitte TD, who always gave credit where it was due.

Danny McCarthy, Adam Brophy, Treasa O'Mahony and all at *Mentor Books* for their help and encouragement.

To *Independent News & Media* for the pictures and Emma Blain and Dave Conachy who sourced them.

To Helen, Mia, Hannah, Georgia and Hugo for everything.

To the one person out there who brought this whole story into the public domain and got nothing in return.

A significant number of people no longer want to sweep issues under the carpet. Every time it happens now they rise from under the carpet.
Peter Sutherland,
Chairman of Allied Irish Banks, 1990

Much corporate fraud is never heard about or published. What you read in the newspapers is the tip of the iceberg.
Anthony L Spollen, Corporate Fraud, *1997*

Chapter 1

A Big Brown Envelope

'Howaya? I've something that might interest you,' said a rasping, familiar voice at the other end of the telephone. After a very brief conversation we agreed to meet. Talking on the phone can be dangerous, even for reporters.

Well built and smartly dressed, he wore a long black coat and when he walked into the pub down on the docks a little while later a thin smile that you could never quite figure out played across his expressive mouth. There was something enigmatic about him. He was part of the establishment yet an outsider and a loner.

'I don't play by the rules. That's why they don't like me,' he said with a smile. He slid onto a barstool and put an unmarked A4 brown envelope on the counter.

I ordered him a pint and we made small talk while we waited for it to arrive. It was April Fools Day 1998. A few lonely punters were watching the racing from Lingfield Park on the television in the corner and nobody was paying anybody else much attention.

When the barman moved away, my friend opened the envelope and took out a six-page document. It was typed on ordinary notepaper without any letterheading.

'I told you about this before, but I don't think you were listening,' he said.

Maybe he had, maybe not. It wasn't the type of thing you'd forget, I knew that almost immediately. Scanning quickly through the document I came to something that leapt off the pages: Allied Irish Bank had 53,000 bogus non-resident accounts containing IR£600 million.

'Holy Jesus,' I said.

This was AIB, the country's biggest company, a gilt-edged financial institution. Peter Sutherland had been the Chairman, James Culliton had succeeded him and now Lochlann Quinn, one of the country's most influential businessmen, was Chairman of a board that seemed to bristle with some of the biggest names in international business. And it was up to its tits in tax evasion.

I turned to the final page: signed by the Group Internal Auditor, one Anthony L Spollen. Whoever he was.

'There's a Pulitzer Prize in this for you,' the man sitting on the next barstool said with a grin. There was something about Dana, a small Irish mining company which had been involved with Allied Irish Banks in raising IR£1 million on the Dublin Stock Exchange. The deal had gone seriously wrong and the bank had engaged in what a senior executive would later describe as 'illegal share support'. But at that moment I didn't know enough about the Dana Affair to fully understand the importance of what was described in the document.

'This is the story,' he said to me, tapping the section codenamed *Octopus*.

He thought that was the most important bit of the document. I'd heard of Dana Exploration of course. They had a tin hut out in Russia somewhere and every so often the shares would take a hike or a plunge on the Irish Stock Market after someone 'in the know' gave 'the nod' to someone who couldn't resist talking about it. Within a few days it was like a tip for a horse that nobody knew the origins of.

But that was how he'd come by it, my friend explained. There was a lot of intrigue involved. A disgruntled shareholder had a friend in Allied Irish Banks and, being a curious type, he'd come across the Internal Auditor's top secret report.

After much persuasion, he had passed on a copy of the document with the advice to sue – the bank hadn't a leg to stand on. It had raided its own Widows and Orphans pension fund, it had artificially propped up the share price to try and save face and, according to its own Internal Auditor, it had brought about 'a disgraceful situation' in the bank and the company.

But I had to look at things in a different way.

Frankly, not a lot of people cared about small exploration companies or the financial skulduggery that went on in them. Most of them seemed to exist only on paper anyway. They might have a shack out in some steamy African rainforest, far from the nearest road and all it took was a whisper and their share price took off as the 'wide boys' went in for another killing.

But banks were different, banks were sexy.

One of the reasons for this was Charlie Bird, George Lee and the tax scandal in National Irish Bank, which the two RTÉ reporters had broken just 12 weeks earlier. Charlie was something of a national institution. Somewhat taciturn in real life, he seemed like an actor who suddenly springs to life when the camera lights clicked 'on' and the *Six One* news became his stage. And George Lee, spectacle-wearing and knowledgeable about financial matters, seemed able to weigh down Bird's more raucous moments and lend them the air of credibility they deserved.

Between them they had taken on the might of a bank, and won. Of course the National Irish Bank wasn't a very big bank. But it was big enough to tell lies and hire high-priced lawyers to defend itself. Yet out of the mire, Bird and Lee had emerged triumphant with a story of financial irregularity.

NIB was a very rotten bank. It was selling 'Single Premium Insurance' to valued clients as a way of taking their money offshore without paying tax. The story had started for Bird in January of 1998 and he would later describe it as 'a poor man's Ansbacher', a reference to the scheme run by Des Traynor and John Furze for Charlie Haughey, PV Doyle and a host of big names in Irish public life.

Basically, the Financial Advice and Service Division of NIB had contacted 'valued clients' who had large amounts of cash. Much like the Ansbacher deposits, these funds were then invested offshore with Clerical Medical Insurance (CMI) but in reality the money was then lodged back on deposit in a secret numbered account in the investor's NIB branch where it was easily accessible.

'The whole arrangement was structured to keep the eyes of the Revenue away from hot money,' said Charlie Bird. 'It was a classic tax-evasion scam.'

One of those participating in that tax scam was Beverley Cooper-Flynn, the Mayo TD and daughter of former government Minister Pádraig Flynn. In time, Beverley Cooper-Flynn and fellow Fianna Fáil TD Denis Foley would play their own parts in the drama of offshore accounts and tax scams.

But the NIB story was just the latest in a series of stories and scandals that the media was breaking. Sam Smyth had revealed that Michael Lowry, the Minister for Communications, had had his house extension in Tipperary paid for by the legendary businessman Ben Dunne. This in turn led to revelations by Cliff Taylor in *The Irish Times* that Dunne had paid over IR£1.5 million to the then Taoiseach Charles Haughey at the behest of Des Traynor.

Various newspapers hinted that Ray Burke got a IR£30,000 bribe from builder James Gogarty, acting on behalf of JMSE – Joseph Murphy Structural Engineers. Jody Corcoran in the *Sunday Independent* broke a string of exclusives about the bribery claims of Tom Gilmartin who gave IR£30,000 to Pádraig Flynn and went on to implicate almost every Minister in the government in his planning scandal.

Banks were sexy, but they were dodgy. They were also robbing their customers and engaged in a huge conspiracy of tax evasion. That was the story that these few badly-typed pages lying on a bar counter were telling me.

Sitting on a barstool looking at them, I began to wonder. Was this as big as he was telling me, or was it just another bit of history that might be better left buried in a filing cabinet somewhere because it would be almost impossible to check out? There was no doubting the authenticity of the document. The man who had dropped it on the counter was gilt-edged. I knew I could depend on him.

This document said that AIB was colluding in tax evasion and cheating on the State and the Revenue Commissioners on a truly massive scale. For years we had been hearing about such things as 'dirty money' sloshed around in the system. But it was usually from drugs or the proceeds of some scam. What I was looking at wasn't evidence of the unwashed money of some crime lord or even grease monkeys operating from a back-street garage. This was a huge Irish bank, supposedly dripping with respectability. These were the guys who got appointed to State boards and went to call on government Ministers when they had a problem. These were the people we were supposed to look up to, the people who kept the country solvent, the people who mattered.

I took out my notebook and began to scribble.

'Don't bother,' he said. 'You can keep it.'

Then he told me the story of how, some time before, he'd been invited out for a drink after work. It was a pleasant evening and maybe they had a few beers too many. He went back to his car and locked his briefcase in the boot before hailing a taxi to go home. The next morning he found his car had been broken into and the briefcase stolen. Nothing else.

He reckoned he'd been followed. He suspected that the document he was now handing to me was what they were really after.

'Have you anything to back this up, on headed notepaper?' I asked, thinking about editors and lawyers. I knew it was the real thing, but I had to convince others.

'Yeah,' he answered. 'I can back this to the hilt with stuff you wouldn't believe. Give me a call when you've digested that.'

Then we drained our pints and walked from the bar as a cold biting wind blew up the Liffey. But it didn't bother me one bit.

The office of the *Sunday Independent* in those days was in Independent House on Abbey Street in the centre of Dublin. You took a creaking old lift to the fourth floor, walked through a set of double doors and down a corridor covered in cracked brown, industrial-style linoleum. Then you descended a few steps, around a corner panelled in cheap beauty board, and you were in the newsroom of the most successful newspaper in the country. It didn't look the part.

The people who read the social columns, and there was over a million of them every Sunday, seemed to think we lived the same lifestyle as those who were described in such detail in Terry Keane's hugely popular *Keane Edge* column on the back page: champagne for breakfast, days at the races, the evening a social whirl and all rounded off in some swanky nightclub. Well, maybe there were people like that, but they didn't inhabit the world of Abbey Street in which mere reporters lived.

A cracked glass door held open by a stack of old phone books led into a long narrow room lit by harsh fluorescent tubes hanging from a ceiling yellowed and stained by water leaks. It was only after you came back from holidays that you noticed that every surface seemed to be covered by newspapers, magazines and books. There were newspapers on the desks and under the desks, press releases and mail discarded everywhere and sun-yellowed files of various newspapers lying on cabinets and chairs. The bins, too, overflowed with paper.

'Don't Touch The Papers' screamed a sign erected by the news editor, Willie Kealy, after some misguided cleaner tried to bring order to the chaos of newsprint lying around the room.

I made a copy of the document and handed it to Willie Kealy.

'Bring that home and have a read of it,' I said and left it at that.

The following morning he sat down and looked me in the eye. 'I don't know where you got that or what it is,' he said, dropping the document back on my desk, 'but it reads like the *Hitler Diaries*.'

He was referring to one of the great newspaper hoaxes of recent times when a German forger 'created' the *Hitler Diaries* and sold them to the *Sunday Times* in London. Not only did he con the *Sunday Times*, he all but ruined the reputation of the historian Hugh Trevor Roper who authenticated them for the newspaper.

The news editor's comment made me think. 'I could get back-up,' I said.

'You'll need it,' he said. 'And if you do we have a story that will sell papers on Sunday. But you're going to need a lot of back-up.' Kealy was pragmatic, but he knew what he was talking about. He was the one who had to deal with the lawyers before and after the story.

'It's going to be a long day,' I thought. I needed this badly, for myself. The *Sunday Independent* needed it too. Something had gone out of the place with the murder of Veronica Guerin, the *Sunday Independent* reporter who had been exposing the dark underbelly of Ireland's criminal gangs and the vast fortunes they were making from drugs. When she had been ruthlessly eliminated on the orders of gang leader John Gilligan, it was like the paper had lost its soul. Many of us had been so busy getting out newspapers in the aftermath of this terrible event that we hadn't actually dealt with her death properly. A colleague, a young mother and in some cases a friend had become another tragic headline. There was an emptiness there; a feeling of indifference to investigating good stories when someone you work with can get brutally murdered because she was just doing her job, a job we had all encouraged her to do because she did it so well and with such enthusiasm.

I looked again at the document wondering what would happen if I couldn't back it up? Would I end up like those old hacks soaking up the sad end of the bar talking about stories they knew but had never written? The ones that got away.

Many a good reporter has made a career out of listening to stories that other journalists already knew, and then finding a way to get them into print. I didn't want this scoop going anywhere else. That day I tried to find things to do, anything but ring the number. Bad timing and you could put someone off for good, but judge the moment right and the story can fall into your lap.

After lunch I called but no success. He was in but couldn't come to the phone. I let it go for a while and then made another call. But now he had left the office and wouldn't be in until the morning. Friday morning was too late.

I knew a few of his haunts and started calling around until I finally found him in one of them, with the background noise of happy Thursday night drinkers getting into the swing of spending their week's hard-earned cash.

'You never called,' he said. I had. He knew it. But who was I to contradict him?

'Can you get me the back-up?' I asked, a pleading note creeping into my voice.

'Yeah,' came the rasping reply. 'How about the morning?'

'That's too late,' I answered.

He wouldn't understand that the morning was cutting it too fine. But I knew you couldn't rush these things.

'Jesus, I need something today. I wouldn't put you under this pressure, but this is a huge story. I've only told one person I can do this, but if I don't deliver it's going to be a big disappointment,' I explained. 'When he saw it he didn't believe it. He thought I'd made the whole thing up.'

'Half five,' he answered, naming the place.

Down in the basement of Independent Newspapers I got out my old black bike and cycled through the city in a thin drizzle of spring rain. I waited in the doorway of a pub as darkness fell and the streets began to clog up with commuters making their way home from work. Vincent Browne passed by in a black Mercedes on his way from the Law Library where he was starting to practise as a barrister.

I waited.

Then, in the distance, I could see the figure approaching,

stooped against the rain and an unkind wind. He pressed a folder into my hands and I could feel the bulk of it.

'Don't let me down,' he said and turned and walked back the way he'd come. The door of a pub opened and for a moment he was caught in pale yellow light before disappearing inside.

I got on my bike and cycled back to the office. In the basement, I opened the folder and there were letters stamped 'Private & Confidential' and littered with the unmistakable logo of AIB.

The letters outlined the saga of bogus non-resident accounts through the letters and reports of Anthony Spollen and John Keogh. There was tension and drama and a lot of turgid details. But that didn't matter. It was all there and the best part of it all is that they all came with the bank's logo and the 'Private & Confidential' stamp. Who could ask for more? It was too wet to cycle home so I went up to the office and rang Willie Kealy. 'We're ok,' I said.

Then I took a cab to the Ormond Cinema to see *Titanic,* the big new movie that week. It was a disappointment. All the excitement I needed was tucked in the brown envelope on my lap.

That thought was in my mind as I walked into the impressive offices of the legal firm of Matheson, Ormsby and Prentice, off Dublin's Leeson Street, the following morning. A big imposing building, soaring like a cathedral, it was a far cry from the dusty solicitors' offices I knew from my travels in Mullingar and Longford.

Gerry Fanning, one of the solicitors who handled the *Sunday*

Independent stories, was already waiting when I was ushered into a plush conference room off the library. He wasn't your typical lawyer although he did have a weakness for those shirts with a white collar and stripes on the body which had gone out of fashion about a decade before, except for the loyal few who were wealthy enough or confident enough not to care that much about fashion.

Fanning was good. He didn't want to know where things came from, what the agenda was or if there was a 'subtext' to a story. He was smart enough to know that if there was a subtext he'd get it, and if the story was true and the documents genuine he'd say ok and it would get into the paper.

He read carefully through the sheaf of documents I put on the desk. When he finished, he looked at me and uttered one word: 'Jaysus.'

He shook his head and told me he wasn't going to ask where the documents came from, all he wanted to know was if they had been stolen. I told him no.

'There's a few fellows down in the Bankcentre not going to get much sleep on Sunday night,' he said with a grin.

Then he took out a fancy gold pen and began scribbling a series of questions on a sheet of paper. We both knew we would never get the answers, but that wasn't the point of the exercise. This was what was called 'covering your ass', or down in the law library: *audi alteram partum* (give the other side their say).

The one lesson they don't tell you in journalism school is that when things get really serious, there is no point in asking a question unless you already know the answer. It wasn't a difficult exercise. All the information was contained in the documents.

The questions all related to the documents and they were all so specific the bank would know that I already had the information. But that didn't matter in this little game we were playing. The questions were simple and direct and, to be honest, I didn't really expect any answers, at least none that would confirm the story contained in the brown envelope under my arm.

Questions

1. Can you confirm that in 1991 the bank had over 30,000 non-resident accounts worth in excess of IR£500 million?
2. Was the bank aware the majority of these accounts were non-resident accounts?
3. Were these accounts subject to discussion with Revenue over a prolonged period of time?

They went on, ten questions in all. Each specific, indeed so specific that nobody could be in any doubt that we already had all the answers.

'Well, by Monday we'll either be in the High Court or every paper in town will be scrambling to catch up with this,' said Fanning with a smile as he showed me to the door.

On Friday morning, at 11.40am, on 4 April 1998, AIB issued the following statement to the *Sunday Independent:*

> In February 1991, in response to a Revenue
> Commissioners' initiative, AIB undertook a review
> of all accounts which were not being subjected to
> Deposit Interest Retention Tax (DIRT) on the

grounds that the account holder was non-resident. The review was completed in September 1991 and resulted in the subjection of DIRT to a number of accounts which had previously been classified as not subject to DIRT. The amount of DIRT paid by AIB on behalf of its customers increased by IR£9 million in 1990/1991 and by a further IR£5 million in 1991/92.

That was it. There were no more answers from AIB.

That evening the editor of the *Sunday Independent,* Aengus Fanning, asked me about the story. I explained it, as best I could. He didn't like complicated stories, but 53,000 bogus accounts with over IR£600 million in them was good enough for him.

'Great story,' he said. 'But I want you in early in the morning to do a backgrounder. This is a big one and we have to give it a good show inside as well.'

It was a long, hard day. In some ways I was learning about the subject myself for the first time. Like most people I had heard about the DIRT tax. Although I didn't have much savings, I didn't think it was a particularly nice way to tax people after they had gone to the bother of saving. But I had never heard of a non-resident account, never mind a bogus non-resident account before.

I should have. Like many people I lived through a time in rural Ireland when local businessmen seemed to pay hardly any tax and even boast about it in the pub. There was a culture in the country that if you got away with it you were a gas man and it was a victimless crime.

It would take Gene Kerrigan to puncture that particular lie. These people were hiding their hot money in bank accounts in Northern Ireland, the Isle of Man, the Channel Islands and the Cayman Islands or in bogus non-resident accounts at a time when Ray MacSharry was cutting spending on health, hospital wards were closing down, accident and emergency services were in crisis and basic services like roads were falling apart. I wasn't the kind of person to work up that kind of outrage, but I was glad to see that Gene Kerrigan could.

The first draft of the story was about the huge liability Allied Irish Banks would have in back taxes as I tried to bring it up to date. But Willie Kealy handed it back to me.

'Start at the beginning,' he advised. 'None of us know anything about this story, so start with the documents we have – the bank's liability can wait for another day.'

I started to write under the heading 'AIB Had £600 Million "bogus" accounts' and a sub-heading, 'Fake non-resident accounts were used to defraud Revenue of millions in tax.' Now it was a question of waiting to see what would happen.

That Saturday night I turned on the television to watch the news and suddenly the first item was the front page of the following morning's *Sunday Independent*. This better be right or we're fucked.

It sold papers all right.

The next Wednesday the following statement arrived, unannounced, with no address or contact numbers, on the fax machine of the *Sunday Independent*.

Statement issued by Anthony Spollen, 8 April 1998:

I refer to recent publicity in the *Sunday Independent* that makes reference to me and wish to state as follows:

My obligation in the post of Group Internal Auditor at AIB plc was to examine the matters falling for my attention and to report on these in an objective fashion and in confidence to the Group Chief Executive and the Group Audit Committee. The expression 'whistleblower' is in no way an appropriate description of these responsibilities or my discharge of them, suggesting as it does a disregard of my obligations of confidentiality.

My reports at all times represented a conscientious discharge of my duties and once they were issued it was for the Audit Committee and the board of the bank to make their own assessment of any exposures that may have been identified.

I have never met with or spoken to your journalist, Liam Collins, nor have I ever provided or authorised the provision of any documents or information to him or any other journalist.

Signed

Anthony Spollen

This statement from the person who was the pivotal figure in the drama acted out within AIB made me aware of just how big the story was. In a country where everybody knew everybody else's business, how had this story stayed a secret for so long?

Obviously, some people did know about it, but it was in their interests to keep quiet. One man, however, a senior figure in the Revenue Commissioners, had been doing his best to take on the banks. He just hadn't been able to find a way to unlock their dirty secret before his own life became engulfed in tragedy and suspicion.

(Except in direct quotes, the letters IR precede all monetary values throughout this book to indicate that the value is in Irish Pounds.)

Chapter 2

James Livingstone Goes to Milltown Malbay

As the chief suspect in the murder of his wife Grace, an event that took place one winter's evening in 1992 in the windswept Dublin suburb of Malahide, James Livingstone would become a familiar public figure. However, before that he was feared only by those who knew him professionally and had something to hide.

A large man with a craggy face and a life-long fascination with firearms, Livingstone had established and headed the Special Inquiry Branch (SIB) of the Irish Revenue Commissioners for 14 years. From 1978, when the SIB was set up in the wake of a series of huge 'tax marches' in Dublin, until the brutal murder of his wife in the upstairs bedroom of their home, he had quietly worked in the background on a mission to track down and punish tax cheats.

A furtive, secretive figure, his job was to tackle the Irish love of evading tax. Like an old-style parish priest with an intimate knowledge of his parishioners' sinning ways, James Livingstone knew in his heart that large sections of the population were hiding 'hot' money in the banking system, away from the prying eyes of himself and his fellow investigators. But outside of that secretive world he was hardly known at all.

In a suite of plain civil services offices in the Setanta Centre, overlooking the cricket field of Trinity College in central Dublin, he would sift through mountains of information in search of the vital intelligence that would nail another tax cheat.

Over the years he had become something of a philosopher on the subject of tax and the people who refused to pay it. 'As long as there is original sin, there will be tax evasion,' he maintained.

He would also insist to younger colleagues that there was no point in asking a question unless you already knew the answer. 'You have to know the money is there and then work back. That is what keeps a revenue investigation pure,' he would tell them.

Unlike a murder investigation, which involves people, emotions, lies and mistakes, a revenue investigator finds the money trail and tracks it back to the source – in the end there is little room for ambiguity in the figures.

In an era when computers were in their infancy and other State agencies wouldn't supply him with data, he amassed millions of single pieces of information. For years a junior in the office would comb the 'To Let' advertisements in the newspapers and then try to track down the owners of flats and tenements around the cities and towns of Ireland. Over the years, James Livingstone discovered that a lot of them were owned by policemen. This became known as 'the blue economy'.

He had a love of acronyms. His mission as a taxman, he would tell colleagues, was SCALPS – Securing the Correct Assessment of All Liable Persons. But he didn't shirk from a fight either and when detectives began to investigate him for the murder of his wife, he began to investigate their tax affairs. He was like that, not a man to give in or give up. Their job was to find a murderer, he believed, and his was to make sure everybody was a compliant tax payer, no matter who they were.

Neither a diplomat nor a 'yes' man, he was largely left alone by his more politically astute superiors because he and his team would regularly 'hit the jackpot', coming up with millions of pounds in hidden money from their investigations. He didn't do it with court orders or police raids. Neither the customs service nor the postal and telecommunications departments would co-operate with him and his work. He did it by the painstaking process of sifting through huge volumes of information until patterns began to emerge. He maintained there was a huge difference between 'information' and 'intelligence' and his quest was for intelligence that would lead to a pot of unpaid tax.

It was this painstaking process that first brought the small west Clare town of Milltown Malbay to his attention.

Jimmy Livingstone had been getting information about the town for some years. Each bit, whether it was in relation to house sales, abnormal spending on 'unessential luxury goods' or simply trends in economic activity, was 'frozen' and filed away as he waited for the right moment. Added to this were GCRs (good citizen reports), that is letters from informers and snoops, signed and unsigned, but all containing nuggets of information. Oddly enough, Livingstone didn't like GCRs but often their information was valuable and sometimes he would knock on a door down the hallway and get authorisation to pay some high-grade informers their ten per cent cut of the value of a tax haul.

****

It was the first Monday in Lent, 1990, and Livingstone was off the drink for the 'Holy Season'. He liked his whiskey but twice a year, Lent and November, he would give up alcohol – although being a man who was precise about figures he would only stay off it for 40 days and if Lent was longer, which it often was, he would ignore the extra bit.

He and four teams with two investigators in each arrived in Milltown Malbay that afternoon. They walked around the town to check out the businesses they would hit the following morning and then, while the others retired to the pub for a few pints, he went back to the hotel to contemplate launching an investigation that would later become legendary in the annals of Irish banking.

A small market town about 20 miles from Ennis, Milltown Malbay is known for traditional music and some fine pubs. In the summer it fills up with visitors who come for the rugged beauty of Spanish Point, a seaside resort just outside the town which takes its name from the Spanish galleons which were shipwrecked on the point and the sailors who were butchered there by the English governor of Connacht, Sir Richard Bingham.

The following morning, as the investigators began calling on the businesses they had targeted, Livingstone casually toured the banks in Milltown Malbay and the surrounding towns. In each he walked up to the counter and cashed a personal cheque. When he was asked for identification he produced his laminated card, identifying him as head of the Special Inquiry Branch of the Revenue Commissioners. He knew that each bank teller would immediately report his presence to the bank manager. It was part of the psychological 'softening-up' process.

The banks were 'bad' and he knew it. He knew of one bank manager who had come into a branch where there was IR£500,000 on deposit and left a year later with IR£6 million in his branch. He had 'stolen' the business from other banks in the town. The question was how had he done it?

The only way this could be managed, Livingstone believed, was by helping customers to avoid paying tax. He knew the banks weren't going to give out any information so he needed the customers to come out with their hands up and own up to tax evasion before he could start going after the banks themselves. And the only way to do that was by frightening them into confessions.

For three days his men combed the town, examining records, sifting through bank statements and chequebooks, questioning the business people about their activities and their undeclared income.

The picture that emerged was of a town stuffed with hidden money, known only to the banks and their business customers. 'I wouldn't say they told us the biggest lies down there,' he would later recall, adding that Milltown Malbay was just one of many Irish towns where cheating the taxman was regarded more as a badge of honour than a matter of shame.

The breakthrough came on the last day. He called to collect two of his men who were interrogating a local shopkeeper and getting nowhere. He found them sitting at the table in the kitchen behind the shop drinking tea with the owner. He began roaring and shouting at them for wasting their time getting friendly with the man.

The shopkeeper began to defend the two tax inspectors and, almost to placate Livingstone and save them from further abuse, he gave him copies of two financial statements drawn on different banks. The following day his accountant faxed four more bank statements to the Revenue office in Dublin. They made further inquiries and eventually the shopkeeper admitted to having 58 bank accounts scattered around the country.

Livingstone got out a map of Ireland and put pins in it to identify each location but he couldn't figure out what the connection was. That evening when he went home to his house in The Moorings, a small suburban estate outside Malahide, the radio was on and Michael Dillon was delivering *Mart and Market*, a daily round-up of cattle prices around the country that was essential listening to every farmer in the land.

Suddenly in suburban Dublin it dawned on him: there was a cattle mart in each of the 58 towns he had marked on the map. The shopkeeper was a cattle dealer and making no returns from the huge profits he was making buying and selling cattle all over Ireland.

After he and his team came back from Milltown Malbay, the Revenue Commissioners picked up more than IR£3 million in unpaid taxes. But of even greater 'intelligence' value was the fact that the local bank in Milltown Malbay coughed up IR£500,000 in unpaid Deposit Interest Retention Tax – DIRT.

Livingstone had discovered that some of the businessmen in the town were using bogus non-resident accounts to hide their money away. They were giving false addresses mostly in Britain and America. Among these was one that cropped up on a variety of bank documentation: 12 Middlesex Road, London, England. When he checked, it turned out to be the address of a Bank of Ireland branch in London. Livingstone knew instinctively that small shopkeepers and farmers in Milltown Malbay didn't know where Middlesex Road was in London. They had never been there and they didn't just dream up this address. It was given to them by the bankers they were dealing with.

Jimmy Livingstone knew from what he saw in Milltown Malbay and other towns around Ireland that the banking system was rotten. The banks were full of 'hot' money and they were colluding with their customers to evade tax. He and his bosses also knew that Milltown Malbay was just another small Irish town where customers had a problem with paying tax. The same thing was happening in Castlebar, Co Mayo, in Roscrea, Co Tipperary, in Listowel, Co Kerry and in Stillorgan, Co Dublin. Tax evasion was rife. Banks and financial institutions were colluding with their customers to facilitate them hiding their 'funny money' in the banking system.

'It certainly did dawn on me, and all our inquiry work tells us that it happens all over the country, that Milltown Malbay didn't have a particular monopoly in this area,' said Paddy Donnelly who was leading one of the investigating teams. 'The plain people of Ireland, I suppose, to put it in those terms, were assiduously salting away their money in various ways.'

'Milltown Malbay was just one town, it wasn't even the worst,' Livingstone would say later. 'Ultimately we would have done the whole country, but Grace was killed and everything changed for me.'

Chapter 3

Main Street, New York

Nobody likes taxes except lazy civil servants and greedy politicians. The easier the tax is to collect the better they both like it. That's why targeting DIRT (Deposit Interest Retention Tax) was so attractive to the Minister for Finance, Mr John Bruton TD, and his cabal of senior civil servants in the Department of Finance.

Ireland was a land of secrets, tax dodgers and fools – the fools were widely regarded as the ordinary working people who had no other choice but to hand over their Pay As You Earn taxes, knowing that the well-padded lawyers or wealthy business people living in the leafy avenues were cheating and dodging like there was no tomorrow.

The Minister for Finance needed money in 1986 and there wasn't much of it about. Or at least that's what people were told at the time. There was a lot more than people made out, but it was hidden in numbered bank accounts, under false names, in suitcases that travelled across the border and in a myriad of bank accounts anywhere from the Isle of Man to the little principality of Liechtenstein where the beef baron Larry Goodman was known to do some of his banking, on account the secrecy laws prevailing there.

So on Budget Day in April 1986, the Minister hit on a new way of taxing people's savings. The tax was already there, but the individuals who were meant to pay it simply didn't bother. What the Minister for Finance did was simply transfer responsibility for paying DIRT from the saver to the financial institution where they kept their hard-earned savings – or, as it turned out much later, billions of pounds in 'hot' money.

This was the real beauty of DIRT or indeed any successful tax. The government didn't even have to collect it. That became the responsibility of the banks and financial institutions where the money was kept. It was supposed to open up a whole new stream of revenue for the financially bankrupt government.

So a clever little loophole, Section 30 and 31, was inserted into the Finance Act. At the time Ireland was almost bankrupt, the best and the brightest young people were fleeing in their thousands every year to the bars of Boston and labouring jobs in London. When they got there and got settled they did what countless generations of Irish people always did. They sent 'the few bob' home.

Some of the emigrant remittances were to keep their families in Ireland afloat. But more were used to build a little nest egg for themselves so that one day they would be able to take an expensive Aer Lingus flight home from wherever it was they had

27

spent the last twenty years and use the money to buy Mrs Mooney's pub in Main Street, or a small supermarket across the road, or open a little back-street garage for themselves. Neither the banks nor the government wanted to frighten this money away. They didn't want it sitting in bank accounts in Boston or Brussels. They wanted it in the Irish banking system where it could be used to try and kickstart the economy.

So, what became known as a 'non-resident account' was created. A non-resident account was not subject to DIRT – because the ostensible owner of the account and the money in it was not supposed to be living in Ireland.

Of course Boyle's Law immediately came into force: for every action there is an equal and opposite reaction. 'Non-resident accounts' soon spawned a whole new industry called 'bogus non-resident accounts' and half the country soon got in on the bogus bits.

It was 'an Irish solution to an Irish problem' in that, while it was illegal to open a bogus non-resident account, those in the know had been told they were untouchable. Nobody would ever find out.

The Department of Finance had secretly obtained an agreement from the Revenue Commissioners on 23 August 1987 that the Department would have to be consulted prior to any examination of forms in which a taxpayer claimed they were non-resident. Of course, years later when an inquiry was established to find out who had made such an agreement, nobody admitted to knowing. The closest anyone got to identifying who sent the Revenue Commissioners' circular to that effect was to blame it on two dead officials – a long-standing practise in the Irish civil service. Always blame it on the dead man.

So this is a typical example of what happened. John Joe MacMurphy, a man running a profitable newsagents in Tralee, had a 'private' account in a bank in the town. A little bit of his hard-earned cash went into the account unknown to the taxman and everyone else. He was building his nest egg for the future. Then, in 1987, he looked at his yearly bank statement and noticed that there was a heavy deduction under the heading of 'Deposit Interest Retention Tax'.

John Joe wasn't pleased and he wasn't long about going down to the bank and asking to see the manager. 'What's this?' he inquired when he had gained an audience in the inner sanctum of the manager's wood panelled chamber.

'Ah the government, the feckers, are turning us into tax collectors, Johnny. It's Mac the Knife's new tax, a tax on people's savings. But there's nothing to be done about it now, it's passed into law and all that. But don't worry, your account is going well and interest rates are good, you'll be all right in the end.'

John Joe protested a bit more but it didn't do him a whole lot of good. Later that week he was taking a constitutional along Denny Street one night and he saw a light twinkling in the upstairs window of the Chamber of Commerce. So, up the stairs he goes and into the cosy little bar that they have there for members and their friends, the kind of people who didn't like to be pestered about business matters when they were out for a drink, or maybe didn't want to be seen taking a drink by their employees and so avoided the pubs.

John Joe sits up on a high stool at the bar. He recognises the young fella sitting on the stool next to him. A good young lad, a bank official, didn't he stay in the house with them as a lodger a few years back when he first arrived in town.

'Will you have a pint?' he asks and Fergus, the bank official, is only too pleased. The manager in the Allied Irish Bank (AIB) branch where he is an up-and-coming young suit has told them all to take care to talk to good solid citizens, the likes of John Joe, with a well established business and a stake in the community.

One thing leads to another and Johnny launches into a whinge about the new deposit interest retention tax. 'They're penalising us now because we're saving a few bob. It's a bloody scandal,' he fumes. And Fergus looks at Johnny and gives a conspiratorial wink. He knows he has to play this one carefully, a bit like playing a good salmon and just as enjoyable.

He nudges the conversation along for a start. 'You're with the old fashioned bank,' he says. 'A great bunch of lads down there all right. We play a bit of football together on a Tuesday night. But you know, John Joe, they're fierce careful that crowd. Everything has to be done by the book. They haven't gone on some of the courses I've been on, finding innovative ways of looking after their customers.'

John Joe looks at him shrewdly. 'Innovative?' he asks. 'What does that mean?'

'Ah John Joe, can I let you in on something that's not widely known? They're not telling people about this but I can tell you it's 100 per cent true. This auld DIRT thing only applies to people who are resident in the country all the time. Now, if you were to open an account with us and have an address that wasn't in Ireland, in the 26 counties say, then that account wouldn't be liable for DIRT tax.'

John Joe looks at his friend with interest. 'But you know that I do live right here in the Republic of Ireland. And right here in Tralee at that,' he says, just to make sure he was getting the drift of the conversation right.

'Ah that's true. But the beauty of this thing is you come in to me and I'll open the account. And you'll have to fill in a few forms of course. One of them is an auld thing called a Form F which has your address and you have to say you don't live in the jurisdiction. But here's where it gets good. I don't have to show that Form F to anyone. It's like a secret. The Revenue Commissioners are not allowed to look at the Form F because the right people, the politicians and the bigwigs in the Central Bank, have told them not to. How do you like that?'

'Where's the catch?' asks Johnny.

'Well there is a small catch. You see, if you don't live here the bank isn't going to be making as much money on your account as it would on a normal one, so we're practically losing money on this. So the interest is one per cent less than on your ordinary account. But the thing is that's more than paid for by the fact that you're not paying the DIRT tax.'

John Joe finishes his pint and walks back along Denny Street, past the dark silhouette of the Pikemen commemorating the heroes of 1798. It doesn't take him long to make up his mind.

A couple of days later young Fergus gets a call to go to the counter where John Joe is waiting. 'I'm here to sign up for one of those non-resident accounts you were telling me about,' he says conspiratorially.

'Fine,' says Fergus and he winks at the assistant manager as he goes past him to the filing cabinet to draw out a wedge of forms.

John Joe signs on the dotted line on every document that's put in front of him. Until he comes to the Form F. Then he looks up at Fergus who manages to be looking away. He thinks briefly when he comes to the box marked 'Address'.

Then he prints his name and address in block capital letters: 'John Joe MacMurphy, Main Street, New York, America.'

Fergus looks down and raises an eyebrow. 'Were you ever in America?' he asks with a smirk.

'I was.'

'What part?'

'North,' the shopkeeper answers economically. Then he turns and walks through the door and out into the street with a big smile on his face. It's a smug smile that will stay on his face for more than a decade as he watches his account grow and blossom. And he isn't the only one to come calling on Fergus, lured by the promise of a tax free non-resident account. Fergus is damn good at selling it and soon he is climbing the corporate ladder in Allied Irish Bank, being noticed in high places and promoted to the Divisional Headquarters because of all the business he is bringing in. (Note: John Joe's story is a generic example of how bogus non-resident accounts were set up; it is not an historical record, although in one famous case an account holder did give his address as 'Main Street, New York'.)

But then, ten years later, when the accounts had been swollen and fattened by a booming economy and the lack of tax, the smile is suddenly wiped from a lot of faces on a Sunday morning in April.

But all that is in the future. In the meantime, John Joe MacMurphy and thousands like him, up and down the length and breadth of Ireland, become members of a secret, clandestine organisation, known only to themselves, their bankers and the Revenue Commissioners.

They are the holders of bogus non-resident accounts.

****

During all those years the people in this big, bright, golden circle maintained a conspiratorial silence. The secret was safe with the bank. They know so many things about people's private lives and they like to keep them buried safely like the gold bullion in their vaults.

But as Peter Sutherland, the patrician Chairman of Allied Irish Banks, would often remind people – things that are swept under the carpet have a dreadful habit of suddenly reappearing when least expected. Funnily enough, Peter Sutherland shared a lot of secrets and one in particular had cemented a bond between himself and his childhood friend Anthony Spollen. They were such good friends indeed that they never mixed business with pleasure, but when they finally did, the consequences were catastrophic for many people.

Wicklow County Council
County Library Services

Chapter 4

A Culture of Greed

Sitting in his small study just inside the main door of Abbeville, Charles J Haughey waved his arm in contempt at the mention of Allied Irish Banks. He despised those who feared him, lent him money and then whinged about it when he wouldn't pay them back. The bank had allowed the profligate Haughey, who lived in an imposing Gandon mansion on his Abbeville estate in north Dublin, so much money that by the time he rose to the position of Taoiseach he owed them IR£1.4 million.

It was a lot of money in 1979. It was later calculated that this debt was about €15 million in today's money, a staggering amount for one man, especially a politician on a relatively small salary, to owe to a bank. The debt with AIB was a well-kept secret among senior bankers and 'movers and shakers' in Dublin's financial circles as Haughey haggled with the bank to have much of it written off.

This task was left to his oily accountant, Des Traynor. He was the one who took personal pleasure in sorting out the tangled financial affairs of 'The Boss' as Haughey was known. Traynor was a remarkable man. He was Chairman of the building conglomerate Cement Roadstone Holdings (CRH) and a director of Guinness & Mahon Bank in Dame Street, Dublin, where he kept what were known as 'the Ansbacher deposits'. These were funds from wealthy Irish clients which were held in the Guinness & Mahon Cayman Trust (GMCT). Yet he appeared to have no office or secretarial staff. He was a private banker to those 'in the know' in the hidden Ireland of the late 1970s and 1980s.

If you wanted to deal with him, and all the 'best' people in Dublin at the time did, you caught up with him in the foyer of the Burlington Hotel where he had morning coffee and held court. Alternatively, you could be given an introduction at one of the small number of social functions such as Stock Exchange dinners attended by the great and the good of the small, tightly-knit Dublin financial establishment. If he took you on as a client you became a secret number in a little black book that appeared to be his only filing system.

Because Des Traynor knew about Charlie Haughey's troubles with Allied Irish Bank, so did a number of serious 'players'. Michael Smurfit was a member of the board of AIB. So was Jim Culliton, a colleague of Traynor's in CRH. PV Doyle, the hotel owner and businessman, was a confidant of Traynor's and one of the secret numbers on his client list. Unfortunately for Haughey, Ben Dunne, the supermarket and retail tycoon, also knew about his money troubles. Indeed, Dunne told Traynor, who came to solicit a contribution from him, that he was so concerned about the trouble 'The Boss' was in that he decided to write IR£750,000's worth of cheques so that Traynor could clear the debt. Why entrust such a sensitive decision to four or five different people, he said, when he could deal with it with the stroke of a pen. The money, he believed, would never be traced. 'Even Jesus had a Judas, so why tempt fate?' he told Traynor.

How wrong both of them were!

So the secret was safe, for the time being at least. It was in all their interests to keep it so, but it was the sort of thing that powerful people savour, knowing that some day, at some time in the future, such information might come in useful.

Someone did try to let it out. When Haughey became Taoiseach for the second time in 1987, a journalist called Des Crowley, who was working in the newsroom of *The Irish Press*, was told that Haughey had a large debt with the bank. The story got into the early editions of the *Evening Press* at the time. Allied Irish Banks immediately issued a categorical denial that the story was true and it was pulled. Oddly enough, the Press Officer of AIB, Bob Ryan, claimed that he never issued that press release and, surprisingly, he never found out who did.

Although his contempt for AIB was manifest, when you tried to nudge Charlie Haughey into talking about his dealings with the bank he would give an imperious wave of his hand and move the topic elsewhere. There were too many painful memories in it for him. 'Dreadful shower of bastards' was as far as he would go, sentiments that were often echoed by more law-abiding people than the elderly Haughey.

Allied Irish Banks was a curious amalgam of rural Catholic

greed, brilliance, brashness and sheer buccaneering in a world that was then largely dominated by Protestant reserve and reticence. The bank was born out of a merger, finally concluded on 21 September 1966, of three Irish banks: The Munster & Leinster Bank, The Provincial Bank and The Hibernian Bank, which had been founded by Daniel O'Connell.

The founding directors of the new conglomerate were Edmond 'Mon' O'Driscoll, John William Freeman, Patrick Burke, David Coyle, Desmond Butler, Declan Dwyer, Brendan Harty, Robert Druitt Langan, Frederick Moore, Charles Francis Murphy, Samuel Thompson and Niall Crowley. There was a strong 'Munster' influence among the founding directors that continues in the bank to this day. But by the time of the events to which we are coming, Niall Crowley, from a well-known Dublin business family, was the only remaining member of the original board.

He was a director from 1966 until he handed over as Chairman in 1988 to Peter Sutherland. A mutual friend of the two men, and one of Sutherland's great friends since they were classmates at a prestigious Jesuit college, was the Group Internal Auditor of AIB, Anthony L Spollen.

At a time when the Dublin financial institutions, stock-broking firms and stock exchange were dominated by scions of the ascendancy who had a more leisurely attitude to high finance, AIB was shaking off its Catholic guilt and embracing a 'greed is good' philosophy which would change the Irish financial landscape forever. Among the early executives' strategies at the bank was to lure influential customers – so-called 'Key Business Influencers', or 'KBIs' as they were referred to, onto its books.

And so it managed to get as clients two successive and very different Irish political leaders, Charles J Haughey and Garret FitzGerald. Ironically, in the years that followed it would have to write off considerable sums of money for both of them.

When 'Charlie' became Taoiseach in 1979 he was in negotiations with AIB about his staggering overdraft of IR£1.4 million. From December 1979, when he became Taoiseach, until January 1980, Mr Haughey's trusted lieutenant Des Traynor negotiated with senior figures in the bank, Chairman Niall Crowley and Deputy Chief Executive Paddy O'Keefee, about arriving at a settlement.

Haughey, living the life of a country squire with his mansion, his horses, his mistress, his yacht *The Celtic Mist* and his Charvet shirts ordered specially from Paris, simply refused to pay back what he owed the bank. Various figures were thrown back and forth and finally Mr Traynor agreed that Mr Haughey would pay back just IR£750,000, leaving the bank to write off around IR£500,000, which was an enormous sum at the time. There was the promise of a further IR£110,000. It became known as a 'debt of honour' because under the agreement reached with the bank, Haughey 'verbally' agreed that when times got better he would repay this money. But once he got the bank off his back, 'The Boss' never bothered. He treated AIB with the disdain which he believed they deserved. As if to prove he was right, the bank never sought repayment of this 'debt of honour'.

The other main plank of the AIB business strategy was to diversify outside Ireland by investing in the international markets. That is how, in 1983, AIB came to own the Insurance

Corporation of Ireland (ICI). This disaster has been well documented, but it was probably one of the most astonishing episodes in Irish business. More importantly it gives a unique insight into the greed and dishonesty at the heart of Ireland's biggest financial institution.

In October 1984, AIB realised that its recent acquisition, ICI, had racked up such vast and unquantifiable losses on the London insurance markets that it was threatening the entire future of the bank. Among the directors of ICI when the disaster struck was the newly appointed Chief Executive of AIB, Gerald B Scanlan, or GB as he signed himself on bank documents. Educated at the Dominican-run Newbridge College in Co Kildare, he had worked his way from the lowly position of bank clerk in the Munster & Leinster Bank to the very top of the executive ladder.

Now, as Chief Executive of AIB and a Director of ICI, he was the man faced with a disaster which could end his career and destroy the bank.

In the week leading up to St Patrick's Day, 17 March 1985, Niall Crowley and Gerry Scanlan approached the government to inform them of the calamity facing the bank. They claimed it could bring down the entire Irish financial system. According to Garret FitzGerald, who was Taoiseach at the time: 'I was temporarily laid up' and the matter was handled by his Minister for Finance, Alan Dukes TD, and the Minister for Industry and Commerce, John Bruton TD.

However, Charlie Haughey, leader of the opposition Fianna Fáil party, had a different recollection. He didn't know where Garret was, but he remembered distinctly taking a phone call from him on the matter as the crisis deepened that week.

In any event, it was announced in Dáil Éireann on Friday, 15 March, that the Irish government had bought ICI from the bank to save AIB from collapse. The Central Bank of Ireland was to work out a scheme of how to finance the purchase.

The deal done, AIB Chief Executive Gerry Scanlan promptly bought 50,000 shares in AIB at a discount price. He then had the gratification of seeing them rise in value by 25 per cent before the Central Bank announced the financial package to rescue ICI.

This consisted of a complicated scheme whereby AIB would make a low interest loan to the Central Bank of Ireland and it would be supplemented by a levy on all the financial institutions in the country. This package was not generally known about until March 27, several days after Scanlan bought his shares in the bank.

The Labour Party politician Barry Desmond said later that he believed the board of AIB had behaved 'in a cavalier fashion' and had been involved in the transfer of shares which was 'questionable' at the very least. These allegations, like the scandals that would beset AIB over a decade later, were never properly investigated and no action was taken against the bank by the various regulators.

Within weeks of being bailed out of this disaster, AIB announced that it would be paying shareholders a substantial dividend and the Managing Director, Niall Crowley, even had the audacity to say that the disaster had been a worthwhile experience for the bank. 'We learned a lot and it brought out the best in us . . . we came through it, and that alone was a great counterweight to the pain we'd suffered. We've gone from strength to strength ever since and gained confidence as a result.'

But those who felt they had been 'conned' into rescuing AIB were not impressed by the bank's subsequent behaviour.

'I wasn't very happy with the way AIB handled it. They told us there was a terrible crisis and all the rest of it but then they increased the dividend afterwards . . . very embarrassing for us,' said the usually mild mannered Garret FitzGerald. 'I was unhappy with the way they handled it but I don't think taking a stake in it was sensible. I remember when Haughey suggested that and I just thought it was the wrong approach.'

In his autobiography *All In a Life*, FitzGerald maintained he was 'shocked at the provocative way in which the bank' had sucked in the government and then walked away from this disaster.

What he didn't say was that it was also a tribute to the steel nerves of Niall Crowley and Gerry Scanlan in AIB. By sheer brinkmanship they had panicked FitzGerald's government into intervening in a business disaster which saved their skins. Ultimately, customers of AIB and its rival banks and the taxpayers had to pay for AIB's disastrous foray into the international insurance market through the 'banking levy'.

At least Charlie Haughey gauged the public mood on the issue. 'It would be an absurdity, an unacceptable injustice and totally ridiculous if the general public, the great majority of whom have never benefited one iota from banking profits and many of whom have had a very unhappy experience at the hands of bankers, were asked to step in and take up an additional burden because of someone else's mistakes, mistakes made in this very specially privileged sector of our economy,' he said, opposing the government's rescue measure.

Haughey was also letting the bosses in AIB, and particularly its Chief Executive, GB Scanlan, know that when it came to his own personal overdraft he would be just as ruthless with them as they had just been with the government.

The ICI debacle cost an estimated IR£357 million and as late as 1992 AIB got a further injection from the State of IR£32 million. It was Albert Reynolds, when he became Taoiseach, who finally called in the Chairman of AIB, Peter Sutherland, and demanded that the bank, which had grown prosperous and fat in the intervening years, should pay back at least a portion of the money from the ICI disaster.

In the meantime, Garret FitzGerald, who had authorised the rescue of ICI, borrowed IR£250,000 from AIB to buy shares in GPA – the aircraft-leasing firm owned by businessman Tony Ryan who seemed set on world domination of the skies. FitzGerald and his good friend and one-time legal/political advisor, Peter Sutherland, were Directors of GPA, but while FitzGerald borrowed heavily to buy a stake in the Shannon-based aircraft-leasing company in the run-up to its public flotation on the stock markets, the wily Sutherland bought only a token share and did not borrow any money to do so.

When GPA collapsed spectacularly on the eve of the venture, FitzGerald was among those left with huge debts. After negotiations some years later, he agreed to pay back IR£50,000 with the bank writing off more than IR£200,000, also a considerable sum at the time. Curiously, Garret FitzGerald never involved Peter Sutherland in his troubled financial affairs, even though his good friend was now Chairman of the bank.

Or so he said.

'No, I don't think Peter Sutherland was aware of it,' he said about his own 'debt of honour' in 1999 when the matter became public knowledge. 'My recollection is that contact was made at bank level, by executives of the bank. As far as I can recall I don't think I spoke to Peter about it. He knew about it. I could be wrong about that, it is difficult to recall six years later. Certainly he had no involvement; it was negotiated at the level of bank officials.' The contrasting debts of Haughey and FitzGerald were later referred to in a typically biased editorial in *The Irish Times*: 'Ungraciously AIB went after Garret FitzGerald in 1994 when he owed them several thousand pounds following the collapse of GPA. Garret, unhappily, did not have the chutzpah of his political rival, Charlie Haughey, to tell AIB what do to with itself.' By then AIB was already proving the old adage that 'a good deed never goes unpunished'.

Even as the State was bailing out the bank, its executives, staff and customers were already perpetrating a tax scam that would cost the Irish State hundreds of millions of pounds at a time when the country could least afford it.

But for a series of unfortunate events it would have got away with that scam too. Luckily for the taxpayers, even banks sometimes get caught out.

Chapter 5

Two Little Boys

In the beginning they were two little boys. The year is about 1954. Throughout those long hot summers of childhood they would lounge together on the grass, play cricket or just idle all the livelong day, as eight-year-old boys do. They went on to be school friends at Gonzaga College, that Jesuit bastion of learning and upper-middle class privilege in Ranelagh, then on the fringes of Dublin city.

They were very different in their own ways, yet typical products of their time in Ireland, then a sleepy backwater on the edge of Europe. Peter Sutherland, the gregarious boy, almost obsessive about rugby, bookish without being the school swot. Anthony Spollen, remembered by school friends as a much quieter figure, less willing to mix, content with his own company yet a hard worker determined to fulfil the promise that was expected of him.

Their fathers too were part of a small but prosperous clique at a time when most people were said to be 'poor but happy', when emigration was the safety valve that kept the country from revolution, when people minded their own business and Eamon de Valera and Archbishop John Charles McQuaid gave them values for life. WG Sutherland, Peter's father, was a prosperous insurance broker who lived in what was then an outer suburb of Dublin, Monkstown. Spollen's 'dear old Dad', who was given to proclaiming wise homespun advice, came originally from Mayo and the family lived in Ranelagh where he ran a thriving pharmacy.

During the summers the boys would spend time in each other's homes and were generally known as good friends who kept in contact, maybe not always as closely as they would have liked, when their paths diverged after school. But the two young boys who grew up together would turn into two very different men before eventually working together in Allied Irish Banks. According to Anthony Spollen, they never mixed 'business with pleasure' but in the end their business affairs became so entangled that they were left with no other choice but to muddy the waters between social life and official business. It was a decision that would prove lethal.

Peter Sutherland read Law at University College Dublin before going on to The Kings Inns where he qualified as a barrister. 'Of course it is very difficult to see oneself but I never thought of myself as pushy,' he would later declare. 'I got important briefs at the Bar not because I was out looking for them, nor as one paper suggested through my family. They came mainly through my own college and sporting connections. Mind you, I don't pussyfoot around when I am in court, that's true. I am tough in debate.'

His friend Anthony Spollen, who excelled at maths and had a good analytical mind, did not go to college after Gonzaga which may seem strange today but at the time was perfectly normal. He became an articled clerk with the Dublin accountancy firm of Forsyth & Co while studying accountancy at night in Rathmines College of Commerce.

His first boss was Alex Spain who would become a close friend and mentor to the young Spollen. Over the next twenty years their paths would cross frequently in the small tightly-knit world of Dublin big business, where secrets were known and kept with a seal of honour.

When Forsyth & Co merged with Stokes Kennedy Crowley, Anthony Spollen already knew Niall Crowley who would become his self-confessed 'best friend' in later life. Crowley went on to become Chairman of Allied Irish Banks before Peter Sutherland and would die not knowing the secret of why Anthony Spollen left the bank so suddenly in July 1991. But all that was in the future.

When he qualified as an accountant in 1969, Anthony Spollen joined the then newly-formed Allied Irish Banks (AIB). There he would work for the next 22 years, a loyal servant who worked his way through the ranks from a junior executive to one of the most senior figures in the bank. AIB was run like a military organisation, where people obeyed orders without question, consorted within their own rank and always sought to placate their superior officers, even when they didn't like them or thought them wrong. The man who brought Spollen into AIB was Martin Rafferty, another Dublin 'insider'. Spollen soon rose through the executive ranks at the bank, becoming Financial Controller of AIB's merchant banking wing, Allied Irish Investment Bank (AIIB) where he stayed until he was appointed to the important position of Internal Auditor of the group in 1986.

By then, the friends of his youth were beginning to dominate the business, social and political world that surrounded Anthony Spollen.

Niall Crowley had become Chairman of AIB, Alex Spain headed the B&I shipping company among other things, Martin Rafferty was running the very successful United Drug and Peter Sutherland was among the most successful advocates at the Bar and the Attorney General in Garret Fitzgerald's government.

Married to a chemist (the couple had four children), Anthony Spollen mixed in lofty circles, but unlike his high-flying friends he kept himself very much in the shadows. While not a risk-taker like many of his peers, he was certainly, like Peter Sutherland, a 'mover and a shaker' in the business community. A member of the Hibernian & United Services Club, he was a frequenter of Lansdowne Road for the rugby internationals and a keen golfer, playing with the well-heeled in Killiney Golf Club and with the more influential legal and business types in Milltown Golf Club. He lived nearby in the prosperous red-brick suburb of Rathgar.

By 1986, AIB was still feeling the after-effects of the Insurance Corporation of Ireland (ICI) fiasco and was badly in need of a conscientious Group Internal Auditor, the proverbial safe pair of hands, who would guide the bank through the choppy waters of government regulation. Nobody came with higher credentials for honesty and transparency than Anthony Spollen.

He was, said friends, 'a banker's banker' and 'a man whose code, ethic and religion was complete and absolute discretion'.

But, as with many things in Ireland, a 'safe pair of hands' is often a flawed description of someone who may be too honest for their own good. There were people in positions of power at AIB who wanted someone who would do the 'right thing' in a crisis, that is find a way to get the bank out of trouble, by means of a cover-up if necessary. The last thing they wanted was someone who would find a problem and run to the Central Bank or the Revenue Commissioners or the Department of Finance and admit to it.

Over a decade after he became Group Internal Auditor of AIB, Spollen would write: 'Much corporate fraud is never heard about or published. What you read in the newspapers is only the tip of the iceberg. Why? Because of the wide-ranging and damaging consequences which such scandals can bring in their wake, such as falls in customer confidence, sweeping management changes, board member resignations, regulatory inquiries, share suspensions, share price collapse and massive damage of morale.'

Spollen was writing from first-hand experience as an executive in AIB. But of course none of these catastrophic predictions ever befell the board or top executives of AIB where he worked. Instead they all made millions from executive pay and share options as scandal after scandal washed over the bank.

In the secret world of the bank, confidentiality and cover-up were paramount because if what the great New York hotelier Leonora Helmsley called 'the little people' ever discovered what was really going on, then everybody would be in trouble.

But if he had friends dotted around the boards of many of Dublin's major companies, Spollen had one special friend, Peter Sutherland, at the very centre of power. Thanks to his contacts in the insurance industry and his own self-belief, Peter Sutherland had prospered in the lucrative world of the Irish legal system. In 1986 he was Attorney General and a powerful figure at the Cabinet table. But that did not stop him picking up highly-paid brief fees for advising favoured clients.

The late John Boland, a hard-nosed northside Minister in the same government, told how Sutherland would sometimes suddenly absent himself from a Cabinet meeting. As these were famously long and torturous, Boland didn't blame him. But straying into an ante room himself for a quick smoke during one such meeting, he was quite surprised to find Sutherland being briefed on a big insurance claim that he would be fighting the following day in the High Court. Next door the Cabinet meeting continued interminably without the benefit of his excellent legal advice.

Sutherland was, according to one Law Library observer, 'unusual, in the sense that the older he got the less pompous he became. Normally it's the other way round.'

By the time he was 40, the man who was dubbed 'Suds' by his friends and 'Porky' by his enemies had three lucrative and successful careers behind him. He had been a wealthy and successful barrister, he had been Attorney General and he had followed that by his appointment to the post of Ireland's Commissioner to the European Union. He returned in triumph from Brussels in 1989 to become Chairman of Allied Irish Banks.

From his office on the fourth floor he could gaze down at the front of the bank's Ballsbridge headquarters to a long rectangular pool of water with a tall V-shaped sculpture in stainless steel by Alex Wojert. This sculpture was often interpreted, rather unkindly, by disgruntled bank customers as a two-fingered salute of the kind immortalised by the show jumper Harvey Smith, in other words a message to critics and outsiders to 'eff off'.

Three days a week, Suds' chauffeur-driven Mercedes would take him from leafy Eglington Road in Donnybrook on the short drive to the AIB 'Bankcentre' in the heart of Ballsbridge. The rest of the week he worked as a consultant in legal and business matters.

Once inside the building his security pass would gain him entrance to the special lift which took him to the fourth floor of the complex where he would be greeted by his secretary, Jude Harper. In the inner sanctum of his wood-panelled office all was quiet and fragrant. The large vase of flowers was changed daily with the real world only intruding when he pressed the buzzer or lifted the telephone.

Sitting behind his desk, Peter Sutherland could contemplate a Jack B Yeats or a Sir John Lavery painting from the fine collection hanging on the office wall. Or, indeed, he could contemplate his own good fortune. He was 40 years of age, he had a beautiful Spanish wife, Maruja, an opulent home in Eglington Road and a little place in Goleen in west Cork. He was

Chairman of Ireland's biggest bank with a fat salary and sufficient share options to make him wealthy for the rest of his life. Not only that, but he only had to work three days a week, leaving him plenty of scope for his other business affairs. What could go wrong?

Down the hall was the office of the bank's Chief Executive, Gerry Scanlan, a tough, wiry little man. Unlike the Jesuit-educated Sutherland, he worked six to seven days every week and it was he who had taken the bank through the ICI disaster. He emerged from the wreckage wealthier and with a bank that was stronger, leaner and more focused than any other institution in Ireland at the time.

On the other side of the hall was the Group Financial Director, John Keogh, leading a team of executives that only the best money and prospects could buy.

These three men would pop in and out to each other, as the need arose. They were running Ireland's most profitable business and for them the opportunities seemed endless. In 1990, in the second year of his term as Chairman of the bank, the Irish economy may have been sluggish but Peter Sutherland had plenty to smile about. AIB's profits were up, business was booming and the bank was leaving its competitors trailing in its wake. So, as he looked across at the heavy, highly-coloured work of Jack B Yeats hanging on the wall, Suds was prone to giving interviews that positively sagged with the weight of his achievements and intelligence. None contained an iota of doubt about himself, or indeed about his wonderful bank.

But if you left AIB's impressive headquarters and turned right, heading into the moderate traffic towards town, just a little way up the road opposite Jury's Hotel you would encounter an ugly carbuncle of a building seven storeys high called Carrisbrook House. It was not fitted out with the same style as AIB headquarters. But it was here, on the top floor, that Anthony Spollen, the Group Internal Auditor, laboured, crunching the numbers that were vital to the future of the bank.

Spollen was discreet. So discreet that even John Keogh, nominally his boss and the Group Financial Director of AIB and a 'friend' who had joined the bank at the same time, was not aware of the bond of friendship that existed between Spollen and Sutherland stretching back to their school days.

'In the middle of December 1990, Mr Sutherland phoned me to say that he and Mr Culliton (another director of AIB) had been discussing the Group Internal Auditor and his rank. I was very surprised because it's most unlike Mr Sutherland, [he] never interfered. We were friends literally since I was the age of eight . . . he was my oldest friend. We went to Gonzaga College, we were terrific friends all our lives and whenever he had difficulties in his life, I was there and vice versa. We were good friends,' recounted Mr Spollen.

'When he became Chairman of the bank in 1989, we had this understanding we would not discuss AIB and its internal matters. We'd go out socially a great deal but we just did not [talk bank business] and that was because he is very professional, a very decent man who knows the way things should be done. In this instance, he called me about ten days before Christmas and said he and Mr Culliton had had a chat and they felt that the group internal audit department should be uplifted.'

In banking speak this meant that Spollen should be promoted and given greater powers than he already had.

This was also mentioned at a board meeting and gleefully recounted to Spollen by John Keogh, his friend on the fourth floor of Bankcentre. And how did Gerry Scanlan take it, Spollen waspishly asked?

'Not very well,' Keogh reported, confirming the enmity that existed between the two men.

Oh yes, what could go wrong?

Little did Peter Sutherland know that his school chum Anthony Spollen had some surprises in store for everybody. While these surprises wouldn't spoil the Christmas party that year, they would certainly make for exciting times in the normally staid corridors of commerce in the coming months.

It all started a few years earlier with a small exploration company with the unlikely name of Dana – a company that had nothing to do with the sweet young singer of the same name who brought fame to herself and Ireland when she won the Eurovision Song Contest with a number called *All Kinds of Everything*. But the song could have proved an apt description of the things that would befall AIB in the years that followed.

Chapter 6

The Dana Affair

John Lord, a man who did not like the limelight, lived in some splendour behind high granite walls and big wrought iron gates. *Inishcorrig* is probably the most imposing residence on Coliemore Road, Dalkey, the affluent south Dublin suburb better know as a playground for rock stars and film directors.

The imposing Tudor-style residence was built at the height of the Famine by the Dublin-born surgeon to the British royal family, Sir Dominic Corrigan. Over the years such eminent guests as King Edward VII and King George V had slept in the upstairs bedrooms. In more recent times, it had been the home of the flamboyant Dermot Smurfit, a younger brother of the packaging tycoon, Michael. Smurfit, who is now a well-known professional gambler on the international poker circuit, sold the house in the early 1980s and Lord acquired the home of his dreams.

Lord, the Chairman of a small oil exploration company called

Dana Petroleum, did not however buy the house for its imposing entrance onto Coliemore Road, although that too was important in a world where keeping up appearances was paramount. No, much more important to the businessman was the private harbour at the back of his house, the largest such amenity in the country.

It was built by the second owner of *Inishcorrig*, Harvey du Cross, who had paid £3 million in the 1880s for the Dunlop tyre patent and was the Bill Gates of his era. He added an imposing tower and finished the harbour which gave him private access to the blue waters of Dublin Bay.

A passionate sailor, John Lord loved to take his ocean-going yacht out into the bay on a summer's evening to show off Dublin's 'gold coast' to friends and business associates. Sometimes senior executives from Allied Irish Banks, with whom he did considerable business, would sail into his personal port for a mixture of business and pleasure. They might arrive on their own yacht and, after a sail around the bay, the bankers and the businessman would dine at the National Yacht Club on the seafront in Dún Laoghaire or in the imposing diningroom of *Inishcorrig*. There they would sip fine wines and discuss the possibility of further mutually satisfying deals.

Between sailing, socialising and his affluent lifestyle, John Lord, who was 43 years of age at the time of these events, had a healthy appetite for ready cash. With a puff of cigar smoke he could dispatch geologists to the far-flung corners of the globe in search of oil and gas. They might or might not be successful. Indeed, for all his flamboyance, Lord more often than not hit a 'dry hole'.

As a result of his less than unerring aim, in the early days of 1988 he and his chums from Allied Irish Investment Bank decided he needed a fresh injection of funds to go prospecting in Russia, the new frontier in the oil business. In May of that year, Allied Irish Investment Bank was enlisted to launch a £1 million share placing for Dana Petroleum.

It was a fairly simple deal. The bank would go to the stock market and sell additional shares in Dana Petroleum. AIB and its investment arm would pocket some very large fees and Lord would end up with IR£1 million in extra capital. But the share placing was an unmitigated disaster. It ended up costing AIB hundreds of thousands of pounds and led to a series of illegal share support schemes. Worst of all, it involved Ireland's biggest bank plundering its own Widows and Orphans pension fund to artificially prop up the ailing share price of what would be known in financial circles as 'a turkey', named thus because it simply would not fly.

The shocking behaviour of AIB and its executives in the scandal has always been kept a deep, dark secret and even when precise details were carried in the *Sunday Independent,* the Irish Stock Exchange turned a blind eye to these revelations.

After what happened in what became known as the 'Dana Affair', Tom Mulcahy, the head of Allied Irish Investment Bank, was promoted to Chief Executive of the bank. The man who carried out the damning internal investigation into how the whole thing turned into such a disaster, Anthony Spollen, Group Internal Auditor of AIB, was shafted.

What made it even worse is that it wasn't just a disaster, it was a disaster followed by a cover-up. It was also the breaking point in the relationship between Spollen and the Chief Executive of AIB, Gerry Scanlan. Ultimately, it led to the uncovering of the DIRT scandal which cost the bank IR£73 million in hard cash, destroyed the reputation of the bank and preceded its tax-dodging customers paying hundreds of millions in back taxes and penalties to the Irish Revenue Commissioners.

What John Lord set in motion on the trading floor of the Dublin Stock Exchange that optimism-filled morning in 1988 would come back to haunt AIB almost a decade later. But by that time John Lord would not be around to learn, for the first time, of how AIB had pulled-off a major cover-up and kept him in the dark about what they were doing. He died of a heart attack one summer's evening as he was tying up his boat in the harbour of his Dalkey home.

'The issue, I suppose, which really drew the line, I suppose, for myself and Gerry Scanlan – and I hate having to go into this – was a failed share issue in AIB,' maintained Anthony Spollen years later when the bank's dirty linen was being washed in public and the 'Dana Affair' was under the spotlight. 'It went badly wrong and rather than face the music and admit it, the bank had been left with an underwriting stick (loss). What happened was the shares were put into the Widows and Orphans accounts, into the staff pension fund accounts. The whole thing . . . the Stock Exchange was never informed.'

The 2.2 million Dana shares (28 per cent of the value of the company) were placed on the Dublin and London stock markets on 31 May 1988 to a 'very hostile reception'. They were placed on the market at £0.45 a share, but because there wasn't enough profit in them none of the financial insiders were interested in buying.

So, Allied Irish Banks organised 'share support'. In other words, they rigged the market so that the price of the shares went up by £0.02 to £0.47, before falling back to £0.33, leaving AIB and its 'supporters' with severe losses. But worse than that, they had egg on their faces from a commercial point of view.

To the top echelons of Allied Irish Banks there was the embarrassment of the financial disaster unfolding around them, but they could live with that. What they would not countenance was the 'loss of commercial image'; a matter of paramount importance for a bank that prided itself as being the biggest and the best in the business. The other financial institutions were laughing at them, and that was far more serious than merely losing shareholders' money.

The following day, June 1, AIIB off-loaded 385,000 shares that nobody wanted into its own staff pension fund and 165,000 shares into its Widows and Orphans fund. These moves were designed to give the false impression that people were clamouring for a stake in Dana Petroleum, when in fact nobody wanted to touch it. A further 12.2 per cent of the shares were hived off into AIIB's own accounts and 2.1 per cent into another bank company.

That night, as the crisis deepened, executives stayed late in the Bankcentre in Ballsbridge phoning 'friendly clients' who agreed to buy more shares with an agreement that if they lost money, the bank would pay them back. Between 3 June and 10 June, AIIB bought a further 5.8 per cent of Dana Petroleum in a desperate, ongoing attempt to give the impression that the shares were worth buying. It was all an elaborate charade.

As it propped up the price of the Dana Petroleum shares, another offshoot of AIB, Allied Irish Securities (AIS), had the audacity to advise valued clients in its 'Investment Focus' that Dana was a 'buy'. In other words, they could make money from the shares.

That August, shortly before its Annual General Meeting, John Lord, Managing Director of Dana, asked AIIB if it was aware of any holding in the company in excess of five per cent, something that he would have to include in his annual report. Allied Irish Securities immediately got on the phone and flogged 800,000 shares in the company to 130 'friendly clients' at a five per cent discount, coupled with a verbal promise that it would buy them back at the price they paid. Then an executive of AIIB got back to John Lord and told him that they were not aware of such a holding.

But when two 'friendly clients' refused to pay for 263,184 shares in Dana, on the basis that they were 'sold a pup', the disaster became too big and dangerous to hide from the top men in the bank. On 10 August, ten weeks after the disaster began to unfold, Tom Mulcahy, then the head of AIIB, went to Gerry Scanlan and the bank's Chairman, Peter Sutherland, and outlined the scale of the disaster.

The following day, Anthony Spollen was called down from his eyrie in Carrisbrook House and ordered by Gerry Scanlan to conduct an investigation into the affair. His instructions were to 'assemble and convey to me as soon as possible all relevant facts relating to all dealings and transactions by all or any of the Group companies in the securities referred to (Dana).' Crucially, Spollen was also instructed 'not to either form any judgement, or make any recommendations as a result' of what he learned during the investigations.

But what Scanlan got from his internal auditor was a scathing denunciation of the business practices at Allied Irish Banks and the various offshoots involved in the Dana affair. Completed and delivered to Gerry Scanlan on 5 September, Spollen's report was entitled 'The Facts'.

What Gerry Scanlan did not want was any 'recommendations' such as the one he got from Spollen telling him that the bank must immediately notify the Irish Stock Exchange and the Central Bank of a whole litany of breaches of the financial regulations which governed banks operating in the State. Spollen was said to be aggrieved at this rebuff from the Chief Executive.

'The conduct of the Group (AIB) in the Dana transaction was clearly civilly wrong and in breach of fiduciary duty,' wrote Spollen. In mitigation, he advised that AIB should openly admit various wrongdoings to the Central Bank of Ireland and came up with the radical proposal that the bank should 'buy the entire company [Dana] thereby bringing about a situation wherein no investor would have sustained a loss'.

For Scanlan and the top echelons of the bank it was an appalling vista. The bank's solicitor, E Rory O'Connor, contacted Spollen and asked him to change elements of his report. He would later say that Spollen appeared to be truculent and difficult to deal with and that he refused to accept that his role was confined to 'eliciting facts' and reporting his findings 'without offering any conclusions or recommendations'.

'I recommended to Mr Spollen the exclusion from his report of an allegation of unprofessional conduct on the part of a firm of Dublin stockbrokers which I considered might be defamatory. In any event the remark was based on hearsay. Mr Spollen did not agree to delete it,' wrote O'Connor in a memo. 'My recollection is that Mr Spollen was in London on the last occasion I tried to contact him. I did not get to talk with him. The message that was conveyed back to me was to the effect that "what has been written has been written".'

As with all major political decisions, if you don't get the result you want from the first report . . . well you simply order another one. Gerry Scanlan now asked the man down the hall on the fourth floor of AIB headquarters, the Group Financial Director, John Keogh, to conduct a second investigation into the Dana disaster. Completed in just seven days, the 'Keogh Report' concluded that 'no notifiable offences had occurred' during the Dana Affair.

The full board of AIB met on 5 December. The 'Keogh Report', and not 'The Facts' as outlined by Anthony Spollen, was presented to them. It was accepted by the board of AIB. 'The Dana Affair,' said Keogh, 'was closed.'

But Anthony Spollen, who seems to have approached his task with an unlikely sense of humour for a banker, was not about to forget the information he had outlined in 'The Facts'. He filed the report away in his bottom drawer and began to prepare a second and far more devastating document. Intriguingly entitled 'Octopus', it would contain not one, but a whole host of allegations of malpractice and shady dealings in Allied Irish Banks.

The Chief Executive and the Group Internal Auditor were now engaged in a battle of wills, and the stakes were high. As Gerry Scanlan would make clear eight years later when it all came out in the wash: It was him or me.

Chapter 7

Ireland 1991

When Raymond John McLoughlin sat down to compile a document called 'A Note to John Furze' in the mid-1980s the Ireland he was living in had a remarkably different landscape to the country we know today.

Most of the population outside Dublin lived in 'two channel land' – which meant all they could see on their television sets was RTÉ 1 and RTÉ 2. Cars were held together by wire and ingenuity and there was no such thing as a motorway. Emigration was the preferred choice of many young people leaving schools and colleges who saw no future in a country with exorbitant tax rates and woeful unemployment.

But of course there was money. It was almost invisible. People hoarded it like squirrels preparing for winter, and they were even more protective about keeping it away from the prying eyes of the taxman.

Governments were turning over so quickly that there were

three elections in one twelve-month period. The socialists in the Labour Party were intent on a wealth tax and the far left longed for a Soviet-style society where everybody would be poor together. The north of Ireland was exploding in every direction, threatening to bring the rest of the country into a bitter, protracted and sectarian civil war. There were tax marches by the PAYE sector who bore the brunt of almost all taxation while wealthy farmers got away largely tax free and the business classes hid 'hot money' in safe bank accounts at home and abroad.

Compared with the rest of the population, Raymond McLoughlin, better known for his exploits as a sportsman, was a very wealthy man. A celebrated rugby player who had captained Ireland and played with the British and Irish Lions, he had settled down to business and accumulated a mixed bag of different companies which traded under the name of James Crean Ltd, a conglomerate listed on the Irish Stock Exchange. A chemical engineer by profession, he was known as a meticulous man with an attention to detail that was rare at a time when the more prevalent attitude was 'ah sure, it'll do'.

He was ambitious, successful and, like must men of his ilk, intent on holding on to as much of the money he earned as possible, for himself and for his family. And that was difficult at a time when the top rate of tax was over 60 per cent and punitive wealth and property taxes were proposed by ongoing supporters of 'the Seventies will be socialist' ideology.

Back in 1976, Ray McLoughlin was thinking about the future. In pursuit of this objective he held a series of secret meetings with other interested businessmen and their advisors, after which he set down his thoughts on paper: always a dangerous thing to do unless absolutely necessary. When his material turned up unexpectedly all of twenty years later, it was a major embarrassment to McLoughlin and some of his friends.

The document was called 'A Note to John Furze' and was to become celebrated in its own way twenty years after it was written as a blueprint for how to take money 'offshore'.

'The material,' he wrote to John Furze by way of an introduction, 'is based primarily on my discussions with yourself yesterday but also to a secondary degree on an earlier discussion with some mutual acquaintances of ours.'

The man he was writing to at this time in the mid-1980s was John Furze, a secretive banker based in the Cayman Islands and an associate of Dublin businessman Des Traynor, Charlie Haughey's bagman. Traynor was at the centre of Ireland's 'golden circle' – indeed he was the man who put it together – and Furze was his contact in the Cayman Islands. He regularly came to Ireland where he was introduced to prominent businessmen. But few of them were as scrupulously careful as Ray McLoughlin and put such delicate matters in writing.

Traynor's main interest in life was in helping wealthy businessmen to avoid paying tax, for a fee of course. His other fondness was bailing out his friend Charlie Haughey who, at this particular time, was watching his overdraft pass the £1 million mark which in today's money is estimated to be about €15 million.

When he wasn't worrying about 'The Boss', Traynor's day job was running Guinness & Mahon, a dodgy little bank on Dame

Street that nobody paid much attention to, which was all right with Des Traynor and his associates.

The other half of the double act was John Furze, who took a personal interest in channelling clients' funds provided by Traynor into mysterious and secretive bank accounts in the 'Crown Colony'.

Oddly enough, both men would die relatively young and unknown, but ten years of tribunals and newspaper investigations would link them inextricably together and leave a lot of wealthy and well-known Irish families wishing they had never encountered this pair of financial wizards.

During the course of his career, Traynor set up Guinness Mahon Cayman's Trust (GMCT) with Furze to channel money out of Ireland to the tax free and discreet Cayman Islands. Some of this money was 'hot', to use banking parlance, but more of it was legitimate. This money was taken 'offshore', breaking exchange control regulations and other rules which Traynor and his friends found inconvenient at the time. To this end, John Furze often arrived in Dublin to meet with prospective clients who wished to avail of his services and take their money out of the country.

Frightened by spiralling tax rates and political instability, wealthy families flocked to the secret world of Traynor and Furze to protect the empires many of them had built up through hard graft and which they now feared would evaporate before their eyes. It was an era when new wealth was viewed with suspicion and avarice, and successive governments tried to claim most of it as their own through aggressive taxation. It was against this kind of background that Ray McLoughlin was thinking about the future and how he would protect his wealth and investments.

It wasn't difficult for a man like him to get in contact with Des Taynor and be put in touch with Furze. They were living in a small intimate community of wealthy businessmen who went to the same schools, played rugby together and appointed each other to the boards of the companies they controlled.

Although he ran James Crean Ltd, Ray McLoughlin was also on the board of Allied Irish Banks. Peter Sutherland, Chairman of Allied Irish Banks, was a director of James Crean and also a director of CRH. Jim Culliton, another director of AIB and the Chairman of its Audit Committee, had spent his career at CRH and was also a director of the company. Des Traynor was on the board of CRH and around this time became Chairman of the company, running it from its imposing office on Merrion Square, Dublin. He also ran his private bank from the same address and kept a little black book with coded numbers and the names and addresses of almost every wealthy family in Dublin at the time. It was all about connections, wheels within wheels.

Even the geography of Dublin at the time was loaded with significance. Walk down Eglinton Road in Donnybrook, Dublin 4, and you would find Gerald Brendan Scanlan, Chief Executive of AIB, in number six, Kevin Kelly, a director of the bank, in 64, and a few doors up, in number 68, was one Peter Denis William Sutherland, Chairman of AIB. The golden circle lived together, played together and did business together.

At that time the favoured method for the very rich to hold on to their wealth was to take advice from Traynor and Furze on how to establish what was known as a 'Discretionary Trust' which would be based in the Cayman Islands. To avoid tax, the owner of the trust could not be a trustee, but would appoint Furze and Traynor (or their nominees) as trustees and they would operate under a 'Letter of Wishes' which the owner of the trust would give them as a form of instruction.

It was a complicated situation because once the trust was established it was not easy for the real owner of the money to allow someone new to benefit from it. The way to get around this was to insert a secret clause in the trust that a person who subscribed $10 to the Red Cross, and could present a receipt for this to the trust, could then become a beneficiary of the trust.

It was to examine the feasibility of setting up such a trust that Ray McLoughlin met with John Furze and Des Traynor and some other advisors and intermediaries in Dublin. Of course, the operation could function smoothly once the person who had established the trust could ring Des Traynor or John Furze and have a pleasant chat and instruct one of them regarding what they wanted done. Things got complicated, however, if Traynor or Furze were not available. How could either party recognise that the other was legitimate in any given transaction to do with the trust? To get over this hurdle they worked out a few secret codes based on passport numbers and other forms of identification.

But there was one other thing that worried McLoughlin. While he was interested in the operation of a Discretionary Trust and understood how it would work when he was alive, he was also concerned about what would happen to the money, most likely a considerable sum, when he was dead.

Going through probate in the normal way was to open up one's finances to public scrutiny and, as Furze pointed out to him, the taxman took an unhealthy interest in the last will and testament of wealthy men, especially those who hadn't paid any tax in the jurisdiction for a number of years.

At the outset, it is important to point out that Ray McLoughlin never availed of the services of John Furze, nor did he establish a Discretionary Trust in the Cayman Islands. But he certainly listened to the pitch from the Cayman Islands' banker. He studied his proposition as only a seriously wealthy and careful businessman might and, in the end, he left us this fascinating document, 'A Letter To John Furze'.

In reply to a series of questions, John Furze told McLoughlin, among other things:

> Therefore at the time of setting out the beneficiaries in the Trust Deed it must be anticipated that any one of those people ultimately benefiting after the client's death would see the list of beneficiaries. It would be important therefore to leave out mistresses and such like.

That too was a reflection of the changing Ireland. The old Catholic order was breaking down, and while there was no such thing as divorce and would not be for many years to come, the stigma attached to marital breakdown was disappearing. In addition, wealthy businessmen were beginning to travel and get a flavour of a new way of life in Britain, America and the continent, where such things as established mistresses were commonplace.

With regard to the money, John Furze had no doubt that if wealthy Irishmen wanted to hide money, the place to put it was offshore in the Cayman Islands. Although, in the end, Ray McLoughlin did not avail of the scheme, many wealthy and prominent figures did. One of the reasons they did so was because they were assured that the secrecy of the 'Crown Colony' of the Cayman Islands would never be breached. Furze continued:

> It is felt that the Channel Islands is more vulnerable in the sense that there is a suspicion already that the authorities in the Channel Islands and the authorities in the United Kingdom exchange information. There are threatening sounds being made by the UK on a continuing basis about altering the taxation status of transactions and entities in the Channel Islands.
>
> If the exchange of information were to become more general there would be a major problem. The Cayman Islands is further away and more remote and there is legislation in the Cayman Islands to safeguard secrecy.

Ray McLoughlin was assured, as other businessmen had been before him, that 'there would be no record of any kind anywhere in Dublin or any reference in any correspondence between

Guinness Mahon Cayman's Trust and Dublin in relation to any Trust arrangement'. In other words, all records would be kept in the ultra-secretive Cayman Islands, safe from the prying eyes of the Revenue Commissioners, investigators or any other interested parties.

Finally, the wealthy Dublin set were warned 'although many of the footprints [that may identify them] can be erased, total secrecy could not be guaranteed'. It was a typical banker's warning: we'll do our utmost to help you avoid tax but if you get caught, we'll hand you over to the authorities without a second thought.

> It is always possible therefore that due to error, or investigation of a sufficiently thorough kind, that the true client might be identified by an interested party as being connected with the trust. On the other hand, if an Irish individual who held undisclosed funds were to hold them to his own account in an overseas bank then it is much less likely that anybody would learn about the matter even though he would be in breach of various Irish laws.
>
> The problem about a tax official identifying through research or investigation who the real client was in the case of any trust arrangement is not that he can claim that the client is the owner of the assets in the trust, because he cannot do that because he legally is not the owner, but rather that

he knows that the assets of the trust arose in the first instance through a transfer to the trust from the client and he will suspect that the assets in the first instance may have been generated by the client without paying the appropriate amount of tax and this might lead to an investigation of the client's affairs of a sufficient degree to track down what the assets might have been.

John Furze may have been a tedious writer but he certainly had a clear vision of what could happen when the authorities began a real investigation into people's affairs. They would find 'hot money' and that would leave the owner of such untaxed money in considerable legal and financial difficulties. But the beauty of the whole scheme for Dublin businessmen is that, in the Ireland of the late 1980s and early 1990s, the Revenue was under instructions not to look at individual bank accounts and the Central Bank, which was supposed to regulate the banks, did not seem to pay much attention to the task.

Of course, many small businessmen did not have the resources to get a face-to-face meeting with such important and influential bankers as John Furze and Des Traynor. Bringing one's money, taxed or untaxed, to the Cayman Islands was by invitation only and so, after the introduction of Deposit Interest Retention Tax (DIRT), the bogus non-resident account in the local bank became the popular method of hiding 'hot money' for the 'ordinary folk'. It was a 'poor man's Ansbacher'.

Like McLoughlin, the small shopkeepers, the bar owners, the

hoteliers and the professional classes, lawyers, doctors and, of course, the farmers, were all looking at ways to preserve their wealth from the voracious taxman. Many of those who wanted to avoid tax in the mid-1980s simply put their cash in a bag and drove across the border, parked in The Diamond in some border town that was conveniently close for them to do business, and opened an account in their own name but using a fictitious address. In those days, before money-laundering legislation, the procedure was relatively easy and the banks were well aware that their depositors were telling them lies about where they lived.

It was no trouble to cross the border with bags of cash. As long as you weren't carrying guns or explosives you were welcomed with open arms into the bank manager's office. Indeed, in many cases, it was the same banking group that held your accounts back in the south.

'I mean, we all used to hear the stories about all the accounts that were held up in Newry,' recalled Dr Michael Somers, a former Assistant Secretary in the Department of Finance and head of the National Treasury Management Agency, the State agency that handled the Irish national debt. 'I think it [the bank] was in the Square in Newry and the banks would send out their calendars to their good clients [in the south] and they would all be returned, person unknown or whatever. That was going on,' he said, referring to a time before bogus non-resident accounts became the favoured hiding place for hot money. After DIRT it was a different story.

'Now it was much easier, of course, if you just had to sign a declaration, you didn't even have to go to Newry then with your bagful of cash,' Dr Somers admitted.

Soon, as another senior financial official in government, Maurice Doyle of the Central Bank, put it, 'the dogs in the street' knew that if you had 'hot' money or you didn't want to pay DIRT tax you simply walked into your local branch and opened a non-resident account. Nobody wanted to do anything about it.

Looking back, the favourite excuse was that the tax rate was prohibitive anyway, so why would people pay all that tax and then voluntarily hand over another 27 per cent DIRT on their savings when all they had to say was they were a non-resident and nobody would ask questions.

It wasn't a bad point, but what would emerge later on, and indeed why so many people would end up contributing nearly a billion euro to the coffers of the Irish government after the investigation was complete, was that it wasn't highly taxed money at all.

Most of it had been hidden from the taxman in the first place and putting it into a bogus non-resident account merely added further to the deception and the greed of those who simply refused to pay tax on anything. So, while tax was prohibitively high for the PAYE sector, most of the money in bogus accounts was untaxed earnings in the first place. Added to that, nearly £2.2 billion in funds had left Ireland as jittery investors took flight, frightened that the economy and the political situation was turning the country into a basket case. Without the taxes from undeclared income that were being siphoned off in the bogus accounts, the government was finding it almost impossible to keep the country afloat.

Sean Cromien, a former Secretary of the Department of Finance, explained:

> From 1987–89 there was a very strong recommendation, that the Department of Finance made, that public expenditure and borrowing should be cut. In those years public expenditure was cut in a quite remarkable way by the government of the time. I was involved in it myself as Chairman of a group, known in the papers as 'An Bórd Snip', where we examined the expenditure of every government department.
>
> In 1992, I think understandably, the government had decided that really the idea that people would pay interest on bank deposits at the top rate of tax was no longer feasible and they cut it back. So, in a sense, that was the atmosphere at the time. Now the danger of dealing with a bogus-non resident account was that you would cause the genuine non-resident accounts to go.
>
> The only way of dealing with it [the problem of bogus accounts] was to give powers to Revenue to go in and look at the bank accounts. That was the only way to do it, and that wasn't on.

But while the Revenue couldn't go into a bank to examine documents, one businessman, Larry Goodman, was so powerful that he could have the Dáil recalled to protect him from the banks. If Allied Irish Banks had been able to stampede the government into buying ICI so that the bank itself could survive and thrive, then there was just one man who could persuade the Taoiseach, Charlie Haughey, to recall the Dáil so that his company could be saved.

Larry Goodman, the Dundalk beef baron, had left school at 15 to start collecting offal and was now among the richest men in the country. But Goodman, who controlled one of the biggest food processing companies in Europe, was having his own troubles in 1991. He had managed to hand over IR£22 million from one of his companies, ABP Holdings, to a Tipperary cattle farmer who promptly transferred the money to Cyprus instead of using it to buy an office block in Blackrock, south Dublin.

Although Goodman was used to doing his business in the vaults of a small bank in the secret principality of Liechtenstein, for this transaction he had used Allied Irish Banks – and it had turned into a disaster. An AIB manager in London discovered, according to Group Financial Director John Keogh, 'that the transfer [of Stg£20 million] was not authorised in accordance with mandate'.

Larry Goodman found himself facing bankruptcy on 23 August 1991. One of his 33 bankers, the Dutch bank Amro, had called in a loan of IR£14 million which Goodman couldn't pay. When the other bankers started clamouring for their money, Goodman, with debts put at about IR£500 million and Ireland's biggest food exporter, was in serious trouble.

Whether he contacted his friend Charles Haughey at his stately Abbeville home or his even more stately new office in government buildings (which had caused public outrage because it had been renovated at a cost to the taxpayer of IR£17 million) is not known. But Haughey recalled the Dáil and passed a special bill which enabled Goodman to go into examinership, and that protected him from his creditors.

In early 1991, as Anthony Spollen was mulling over the IR£20 million languishing in Cyprus, Goodman's bankers came together in Dublin. He had debts of IR£480 million and liabilities of another IR£150 million. But the bankers agreed to a 'scheme of arrangement' which allowed him to write off much of his debts and, within a few years, buy back control of his beef empire from both the examiner and the banks.

In the Ireland of the 1990s, it paid to have friends in high places.

Always regarded as a pawn of big business, Charlie Haughey was a consummate politician. And while he might be parading around the up-market Le Coq Hardi restaurant in his Charvet shirts from Paris and running up large bills eating pike and drinking Lynch Bages, he was also in touch with the discontent people were feeling.

On 3 January 1992, while the rest of the population was still recovering from the New Year festivities, Haughey called a senior official of Revenue, Dermot Quigley, into his office.

Haughey could be quite savage at times, but more often with members of his own party than with civil servants. On one occasion, Senator Don Lydon, who had offended him, was so confused after a 'dressing down' that he couldn't find the door in the wood-panelled office of the Taoiseach. Haughey sat at his desk, ignoring Lydon's efforts for a few moments, before gazing up at the hapless Senator with those hooded eyes and snarling: 'Why don't you jump out the fucking window?' Then he buried his head in the State papers once more.

That January in 1992 Haughey gave Quigley something of a dressing down, but in a more civilised fashion.

'He said, he expressed a view that something would have to be done about avoidance, evasion, enforcement, in the light of recent controversies,' said Quigley later, referring to Haughey's emphasis that something should be done about the banks. 'He emphasised the need to put together measures for the Budget and the Finance Bill that would address the concerns of the Irish Congress of Trade Unions.'

At the time taxes were high, but the average price of a house in Dublin was just IR£67,334. The de Vesci estate, a grand Paladin mansion and 1,600 acres near Abbeyleix, remained unsold for IR£4 million – the cost of a semi-detached house on Eglinton Road, Dublin 4, today. Aer Lingus was offering IR£20 million to take over loss-making rival Ryanair which was costing businessman Tony Ryan a fortune.

By 1992 Ireland was in the European Monetary Union and the sharks began to circle. Currency speculators – many of them prominent Irish businessmen funded by banks like Allied Irish Banks and Bank of Ireland – reckoned that the Irish currency was over-valued and they began to bet on devaluation.

'We had to go around all the banks that we knew and raise cash from them. As somebody said to me, "we tapped",' said Dr Michael Somers, who was advising the Minister for Finance,

Albert Reynolds. All the advice from the Central Bank, the Department of Finance and the special advisors was that Ireland should not devalue. All the big money – and it was billions – was betting that we would.'

Dr Somers said:

> We have always had very good relations with the German banks and we approached them on a one-to-one basis without telling each one that we were approaching the other and we raised from a very large number of them 100 million Deutsche Marks. Now I think each of those intended to syndicate down that 100 million and, as someone rather facetiously said to me, each one thought they had got a pearl of a great price that nobody else had and they were going to syndicate it down. They suddenly discovered there was a string of pearls all over Germany because, I mean, we relieved each of them of 100 million. And we had also to go to some of them and get overdraft facilities of one billion Deutsche Marks – we had two overdraft facilities.

This quest for cash to stave off devaluation of the Irish Pound was known as the '92 and 93 thing' it dragged on so long.

Interest rates were so high and so volatile during this period that businessmen with hard cash, like publicans, were literally moving it from one bank to another on a daily basis to avail of the highest interest rates. But it was also a period when the banks were moving vast amounts of money out of bogus non-resident accounts and into 'offshore destinations' to avail of a secret amnesty they claimed to have negotiated with the Revenue Commissioners in 1991.

But just as paper doesn't refuse ink, banks will always find a home for money. As they closed down the bogus non-resident accounts, teams of influential executives were trawling through the big accounts and meeting with clients. There were other places to keep your money, far from the prying eyes of the taxman but within easy reach of an Irish citizen who suddenly needed to convert their savings back into cash. And these teams emphasised the secrecy that surrounded offshore banking in the Isle of Man and the Channel Islands.

John Furze might have thought that these two secretive destinations were suddenly getting a little bit too close to the British and Irish Revenue. But the Cayman Islands was a little bit too exotic for the average Irish tax dodger in the early 1990s. They left that to the big boys and plunged instead into those little offshore destinations that were within striking distance of home.

As for Ray McLoughlin, time was not kind to the businessman who had once been a shining star of the Irish Stock Exchange. In July 1991, as the board of AIB, of which he was a member, was struggling with its internal difficulties, shares in James Crean were trading at 415p, while the bank shares shuttled between 180p and 190p.

But by the end of the decade the strong, media-shy rugby prop-forward who had played for Ireland 40 times and captained the team to a historic win against South Africa saw his company decline from one of the great successes to a shadow of its former self. James Crean shares fell from over IR£4 a share to less than 27p and it was impossible to stop the decline. McLoughlin eventually broke up the once-powerful conglomerate he had founded.

As if to add insult to injury, 'A Note to John Furze' surfaced when Susan McLaughlin, the estranged wife of businessman Kyran McLaughlin (the head of Davy Stockbrokers), found it in a filing cabinet. Her husband had left it behind when their marriage broke up and he moved to Dublin 4 to live with his girlfriend and their newborn child. Susan McLaughlin handed over the 'Note' to the Moriarty Tribunal investigating the financial affairs of Charlie Haugey and Michael Lowry because of the connection to Traynor and Furze.

Kyran McLaughlin and Ray McLoughlin had played rugby together in Blackrock in the 1970s and, honourable man that he was, Ray McLoughlin owned up and admitted that 'A Note to John Furze' was his document, but he never explained how it ended up in the other man's filing cabinet.

In the end it was just another footnote to the lengths to which the Irish business tycoons were willing to go to take their money offshore – another intrigue in the labyrinth of financial irregularity that was aided and abetted by the Irish banking system at that interesting time in Irish history.

Chapter 8

Shafting Spollen

Friday evening, 18 January 1991, and the bankers were streaming out of AIB Bankcentre heading for Paddy Cullen's public house and other favoured watering holes around Ballsbridge, Dublin 4.

Shortly before 5pm one man was swimming against the tide. Anthony Spollen, Internal Auditor of AIB, was making his way from his office in nearby Carrisbrook House for a meeting with his 'friend' John Keogh, Group Financial Director and a member of the board of AIB.

There was something of a spring in Spollen's step that January Friday, even though he was working late. Jimmy Culliton, an influential director of the bank, told Spollen he had been praised at the board meeting the previous month, the highest accolade a loyal servant of the bank could wish for. This praise had been echoed by his good friend Peter Sutherland who had telephoned him over the Christmas period to add his own pat on the back. The only shadow on the horizon had occurred when a third person, the man he was now going to meet, had told him the same story.

'How did Mr Scanlan react to that?' Spollen asked, rather mischievously.

'He wasn't overly pleased,' replied John Keogh, appearing to take pleasure in the rancour that now existed between the Chief Executive of the bank and his Chief Internal Auditor. Things had not been going well between them.

After the fall-out from the Dana Affair, Anthony Spollen had spotted other problems in Allied Irish Banks which he felt the Chief Executive should be dealing with. But he had been rebuffed by that Chief Executive, Gerry Scanlan, who didn't want to deal directly with the Internal Auditor.

'In terms of my personal time management, it would be impossible for me to discharge my role in the group if executives generally decided to bypass the normal reporting arrangement. In your case, your management reporting relationship is with John Keogh, Group Financial Director, who reports directly to me,' Scanlan told Spollen in a testy memo dated 12 October 1990. 'In the foregoing circumstances the material which arrived to my office recently is returned herewith and I would appreciate if you conformed strictly to our managerial structure henceforward.'

Relations between the two men were now at an all-time low. The camaraderie that had once characterised their relationship over dinner at a gentleman's club in Dublin was long gone.

Now, as he made his way through security and got clearance for the lift that would take him to the fourth floor and the opulent suites of the bank's top executives, Anthony Spollen was in a jaunty good mood. It was Friday evening, after all. A quick meeting and he would be free for the rest of the weekend.

When he got to Keogh's office, which was down the corridor from the Chairman and the Chief Executive, the two men shook hands. They had been friends since joining the bank together as young men. Neither had worked in the branch network but had risen instead through head office staff.

The meeting at first seemed very cordial and the general small talk wasn't going anywhere until John Keogh dropped a bombshell. Anthony Spollen was to be transferred from his position as head of Group Internal Audit and would take up a new position working under the direction of Brian Wilson, General Manager for Ireland, within days.

'We decided to make you head of corporate lending at your existing rank,' John Keogh told Anthony Spollen. He said it was a 'worthwhile opportunity' and a new challenge. But that's not the way Anthony Spollen saw it. He figured he was being shafted.

He was dead right on that score.

There were further shocks in store when Brian Wilson opened the door and joined the meeting. He wasn't playing any corporate games and, in the most direct language possible, he told Anthony Spollen that he was being transferred to a new job and that he had better obey his orders. There was nothing to think about. He would be moved by Monday.

'I wouldn't be pleased with that,' Spollen replied to the news imparted by the two executives as they debated the issue, playing 'good cop, bad cop' with him. Although Wilson's focus was to 'welcome' Spollen to the division of the bank that he controlled, he was forceful in his contention that this was an important strategic move that had been signalled by the Chief Executive and they would all do as they were told. Orders had to be obeyed and Spollen, no more than any of the others, would have to toe the line.

Later, Wilson would admit that his contribution to the executive discussion with Spollen that evening was 'quite assertive and perhaps even threatening'. But, despite the threats and the cajoling, the meeting broke up without Spollen agreeing to anything.

When he left the Bankcentre that Friday evening, Anthony Spollen was angry and confused. Just two weeks before he had been praised at a full board meeting of the bank. He had been told that his department was going to be 'uplifted' which in bank speak meant his role was going to be expanded. Now he was being shafted by some of the very same people who had attended that meeting and joined in the praise. He immediately rang Peter Sutherland.

'Well I certainly became aware of it on the 18th [of January],' said Sutherland later. 'I would imagine that my recollection is that as soon as this issue of the transfer became an issue of, I won't say conflict, but serious disagreement, I became aware of it.'

'I was told either by the Chief Executive [Scanlan] or Mr Wilson or Mr Dowling, the Deputy Chief Executive at the time when these discussions were taking place, and I have a vague recollection also, at that time, of talking to Tony Spollen. I don't even remember whether it was by telephone or directly, about the fact that there was an issue arising in regard to his transfer. And he also raised, if I understand correctly, at the time, orally, issues relating to the matters which were subsequently to become the subject of discussions in the audit committee,' Sutherland would later state.

These 'issues' were the shocking state of the bank's bogus non-resident deposits.

The following day, Saturday, Keogh and Wilson kept in contact by telephone, knowing that their Chief Executive would expect a progress report first thing on Monday morning. They were under such pressure to move Spollen that Brian Wilson turned up unannounced at Anthony Spollen's house in Rathgar that Sunday.

'I felt I was a friend of his,' he later explained. 'Now Tony, as you know, was unhappy about the proposed transfer at that time and I took it upon myself to call to see him on the Sunday. I went in the spirit of friendship, as I saw it. One to try and be welcoming to him in relation to the Irish division . . . to make it clear to him that I felt he could be welcome in our division and that I would be looking forward to having him as a colleague more directly again. And secondly, to try, as I saw it, to stop him painting himself into a corner because the clear understanding in the group was that you had to accept transfers.

'I've never myself been in a job in AIB more than five years and so, you know, it was part of the culture of the organisation.'

But despite the military ethos of AIB, where executives were expected to obey orders from 'superior officers' and carry them out without question, Anthony Spollen had suddenly begun to rebel against the system that he had worked in for 22 years. He was not for turning.

'You have the Chairman of the bank [Sutherland] and the Chairman of the Audit Committee [Culliton] saying I am doing a great job – and you have the Chief Executive intending to transfer me ten days later,' said Spollen. He couldn't understand the contradiction at the heart of what he was hearing.

'When Mr Keogh called me that evening, I just said there comes a point at which you say, you know, you just don't go along with that type of behaviour.'

What rankled even more with Spollen was that instead of meeting him face-to-face, Gerry Scanlan had sent what were described as his *aides-de-camps*, John Keogh and Brian Wilson, to deliver the blow.

When he went back to work on 21 January, Anthony Spollen had a lot on his mind. He knew that his position was precarious but in his drawer he had the Dana Report, known as 'The Facts' and the outline of the even more damning document codenamed 'Octopus'.

Anthony Spollen wasn't going down without a fight.

Chapter 9

DIRT on the DART

One winter's evening, the DART broke down a few hundred yards from Sydney Parade station in leafy Dublin 4. As they glanced half interestedly through the fogged-up windows at the players from Monkstown Rugby Club training a few yards from the railway line, two senior but very anonymous officials from the office of the Revenue Commissioners got to talking about DIRT.

It might not be the type of subject ordinary people would bring to mind on such an occasion, but to two Revenue men stuck on a steamy train it seemed natural enough.

That year Monkstown Rugby Club, on whose pitch the two men were gazing, had won the Junior Cup with a group of players who styled themselves 'The Cult' and whose infamous war cry, 'we are men of iron, men of steel, men of the knuckle' struck terror into the opposition. It was through this combination of terror and talent that enabled the team to beat supposedly superior opposition into a pulp.

The two men sitting on the Dart, Sean Moriarty, a senior executive in the Revenue's investigation branch, and Cathal Mac Domhnaill, Chairman of the Revenue Commissioners, did not contemplate such lethal tactics as those adopted by 'The Cult'. However, Moriarty did inform his Chairman that he was writing, in his spare time of course, a report which basically outlined how the banks were running rings around the Revenue Commissioners on the issue of the DIRT tax and bogus non-resident accounts.

They sat in that railway carriage for over an hour as Moriarty outlined his concerns in some detail to his boss and seemed to get enough encouragement to continue with the project. Moriarty's information from talking to colleagues and his own experience was that the banks were involved in widespread tax evasion. DIRT had always been an unpopular tax with the people who were supposed to return it to the Revenue.

'There was a great uproar from the banks, from Dáil deputies when the DIRT tax was introduced,' said Sean Cromien, Secretary of the Department of Finance. 'My understanding from Mr Alan Dukes was that the Fine Gael deputies were opposed to it,' he added. He also named Dr Michael O'Kennedy, a former Fianna Fáil government minister, as expressing his opposition to the measure.

'If, say, the DIRT tax, when it was introduced in 1986, had extended full disclosure to the banks, to the building societies as well as the banks, right across the board – if, in fact, full disclosure was given there, that would have frightened away capital. So, we would recommend against that,' said Cromien, giving a senior civil servant's view of 'an Irish solution to an Irish problem'. In other words, the Department of Finance had recommended that the Revenue Commissioners could not examine the ownership of non-resident accounts.

His successor in the Department of Finance, Paddy Mullarkey, shared that opinion: 'If you had been able to capture all the bogus non-resident accounts, on our estimation there would have been a yield of something in the order of IR£40 million. We say, as something with a high probability factor attaching to it, the downside in terms of the economy and on the budget would have cost the economy a significant multiple of that.'

Another senior civil servant, Dr Michael Somers, who eventually headed up the National Treasury Management Agency, described the tax take as 'small beer' compared with frightening away almost IR£2 billion in funds held in Irish banks by non-residents.

In other words, 'the dogs in the street' knew about tax evasion, as another senior civil servant put it, but the authorities were not willing to do anything about it because they knew it would frighten people into hiding their money in the Northern Ireland or elsewhere abroad.

'I also worked for 14 years in provincial Ireland and I had a reasonable opportunity to observe at close quarters and, indeed, across all my career, a contact base that you tap into to know what happens in the real world,' said Moriarty. 'But I have to say for all of that, I had very little hard evidence at the end of it.' But when he did submit the paper it was left unread for three months until he sent a second copy to the office of the Chairman of Revenue.

'The Chairman, he was unhappy with the paper, I have to say. He told me there were a number of reasons why he expressed his unhappiness, some of which certainly, I have to say, were valid. He said there was very little evidence for the conclusions I was drawing and, in the light of where we were coming from, I think it is a valid criticism,' said Moriarty later. 'We were plucking at scraps of information . . . because of the fact that we couldn't access the banking records. We couldn't do any kind of sample surveys so we were trying . . . to build . . . a framework of perceptions of experienced investigators that was leading us in a certain direction.'

In one way he was talking about what James Livingstone had uncovered in Milltown Malbay and his firm belief that this level of tax evasion was replicated in towns and cities all over Ireland.

Moriarty's perceptions about the banks, particularly Allied Irish Banks and the State bank, ACC (originally the Agricultural Credit Corporation), were influenced in a small way by the fact that the Revenue's Special Inquiry Branch could walk down the main street of a small town like Milltown Malbay and collect almost IR£2 million in unpaid taxes in less than a week.

It was staggering and it wasn't just the tax dodgers of Clare who were getting away with murder. There were cases in Castlebar, Roscrea and even in the small Limerick village of Doon.

Moriarty alleged that there was over IR£4 billion in non-resident accounts at the time and, going on some of his figures, up to IR£1 billion 'had escaped taxation' and was floating around in the Irish banking system. But he didn't have the evidence to prove it and political interference had ensured that the Revenue Commissioners could not go into banks to examine the addresses of those who were claiming to be non-residents. Neither did his paper, which was an attempt to get Revenue to do something about the scandal, ever see the light of day.

Not only was it rejected, but Moriarty was left with the distinct impression that the banks were so powerful, politically and financially, that they were untouchable. Neither the Department of Finance, the Central Bank nor the Revenue Commissioners regarded themselves as having responsibility for the banking sector. So the banks were largely left to themselves.

'Ok, I always believed that the bogus non-resident phenomenon would stop when the banks wanted it to stop. I am saying that because we had no powers, to a large extent, to make them stop. The core recommendation in my paper is about making an attempt to edge them towards some sort of voluntary self-regulation for the first time, by seeing the whites of the eyes of the chief executives. And the card the Revenue had to play – and I was acutely conscious of this – the card which the Revenue needed to bring to the table . . . was the level playing field,' said Moriarty. In other words, until the Revenue Commissioners could actually look at the documentation, they only had their suspicions to go on.

But another factor which influenced the Chairman of the Revenue Commissioners was that Moriarty was basically advocating an official amnesty so that the whole issue could be cleared up and effectively both sides would start with a clean sheet. (The top people in the Revenue were opposed to a tax amnesty.)

Moriarty was to some extent more pragmatic than some of his superiors may have wished. 'We understand that commercial pressures may have, in some circumstances, been the inspiration behind the bank officials' willingness to facilitate the abuses,' he said in his paper.

As it happens, certain members of the government were also advocating a general tax amnesty and, indeed, when he was Minister for Finance in Albert Reynolds' government of 1992–1994, Bertie Ahern did introduce such an amnesty. In hindsight, it was a disgraceful piece of legislation in that it allowed tax cheats from all areas of Irish life to pay a small penalty to legitimise hundred of millions of pounds in 'hot money'. But that, as they say, is another story altogether.

If Moriarty was coming at things from an academic point of view, then another senior Revenue official, Tony McCarthy (or DA MacCárthaigh as he styled himself in civil service Gaelic) or 'The Boot' as he was known to his colleagues, was adopting an approach more in keeping with the methods of 'The Cult' from Monkstown on the rugby field.

McCarthy described himself as 'a person who consumes my own smoke' or to put it in a less folksy style: 'If I can do something, I'll go and do it.' Others who worked in Revenue around the same time might not have given as kind an assessment as McCarthy gave to himself. But he did reflect a feeling within the Revenue Commissioners that the banks and financial institutions were 'a no-go area'.

It was folklore in the Revenue that officers could not inspect bank documents relating to the addresses of those holding non-resident accounts. And it was true to say that the Minister at the time, Ray MacSharry, had come under enormous pressure from the Irish Bankers' Federation on the issue. He had left one member of the bankers' delegation, Niall Crowley, with the impression that the tax authorities were not allowed to go into banks to check the relevant documents.

This arose from a meeting between MacSharry and the Irish Bankers' Federation (IBF) on 20 May 1987. It seemed odd that the bankers' delegation should include the then Governor of the Central Bank, Louden Ryan, whose job was supposedly to regulate the banks, not join their campaign against the Revenue Commissioners. Following the meeting a memo was circulated in Allied Irish Banks by the Chairman of the bank at the time, Mr Niall Crowley: 'The Minister has indicated verbally at the above meeting that inspectability [of documents relating to non-resident accounts] will not be an issue at any time and provision will be made in the 1988 Finance Act to cater for this.'

However, this memo was unsigned and when MacSharry was questioned about it he denied he had ever suggested such a thing.

'I want to take this opportunity immediately to categorically reject that inference,' he said. 'Almost all the people questioned on this, never once suggested that they had knowledge that there wouldn't be inspectability on this. In fairness to the late Mr Crowley, I would have to say that I doubt if this ever was said by him and recorded in this unsigned, undated minute in the AIB.'

However, there was also the question of an internal Revenue Commissioners' memo called a SIM. SIM263, which came from the Chief Inspector's Office in the Revenue Commissioners 'effectively' instructed staff at the Investigation Branch that there was to be no 'trawl' of 'declarations' from holders of non-resident accounts to see if they were, in fact, genuinely non-resident.

When this matter was investigated, the author of this instruction could not be found. For a time it was blamed on a dead man who, it eventually transpired, didn't even work in that section of the Revenue Commisioners.

As the Comptroller and Auditor General, John Purcell, pointed out in his report, during the period 1986 – 1998 Revenue was not allowed to carry out 'on site audits' of DIRT returns made by the banks and they did not have to power to enter a bank to inspect records.

'I was very cognisant of the fact that the banks were effectively a no-go area so what I wanted to do then was – I felt the matter should be tackled, and tackled in a way where the banks would co-operate,' Tony McCarthy said later.

McCarthy, who was a senior executive in the investigation branch, had two tax fraud cases, both involving AIB. He wrote them a 'stern letter' on 31 December 1990 demanding a meeting to discuss the bank's 'compliance record' in tax matters.

The senior figure in the AIB tax department, Jimmy O'Mahony, was a former senior member of the Revenue Commissioners' staff who had been 'poached' by the bank. They agreed to a meeting on 5 February 1991 to discuss the issue. But, at the last minute, the meeting was suddenly deferred by Mr O'Mahony on behalf of the bank. It has never fully emerged why the meeting was postponed. But, because of the internal strife in AIB at the end of January, there was a distinct feeling at senior executive level that somebody in the bank may have been leaking details of what was happening to the Revenue.

What the Revenue Commissioners didn't know, and could not have known at the time, was that Anthony Spollen, Group Internal Auditor of AIB, had suddenly discovered the 'appalling vista' of bogus non-resident accounts at the bank. There was a huge upheaval going on in the bank from Peter Sutherland down.

'The estimates for bogus non-resident accounts which you have given me are frightening,' Spollen told his fellow AIB internal audit executive, Don Walsh. 'This whole matter has, I believe, very serious implications for AIB and we must quantify both the potential liability arising from what has taken place to date and ensure that the bank is protected against these types of deposits in the future,' he said.

Even as he was writing the memo, dated 30 January 1991, alarm bells were beginning to sound among the higher echelons of the bank.

Jimmy O'Mahony, a man who enjoyed shooting and fishing and was known as 'The Pheasant', and Deirdre Fullen, the two most senior officials in the bank's tax department, finally met with AIB's 'Head of Branches', Pat O'Mahony, on 31 January to try to find out the exact position so that they could get their story straight before the meeting with Revenue.

When it did finally take place at Revenue offices in Nassau

Street, Dublin, on 13 February 1991, the meeting, which was originally a meeting about two cases of tax fraud at AIB, became a much wider discussion about the whole performance of the bank in relation to its returns of Deposit Interest Retention Tax. In the intervening week McCarthy had said he wanted to 'widen the discussion' so that Jimmy O'Mahony and Deirdre Fullen from AIB were even more nervous going into the meeting, thinking that the Revenue Commissioners were somehow tapping into what was happening in AIB.

The bank's top executives knew they had a major problem but were intent on keeping it secret, while the Revenue Commissioners knew there was something up within the bank but didn't know what it was and couldn't find out.

McCarthy, the taxman, knew they were hiding something from him, but it was only a 'smell', he didn't have any hard evidence beyond two separate cases of tax fraud. As he would say later in a scorching indictment of AIB: 'This whole case has been riddled with deceit.'

He had a hunch and, like any good investigator would, he decided to act on it. As he walked along the corridor to the meeting he literally 'rounded up' three other Revenue officials and dragged them into the meeting to intimidate the bankers.

He was the 'gunslinger' and Liam Liston, Paddy Donnelly and Dan Roddy were the back-up, even if Donnelly would later admit, 'we were shooting in the dark.'

'It was a psychological confrontation,' said McCarthy, recalling the event. 'The truth is that overall we only knew a small number of cases. We had our suspicions, we had a gut feeling, but overall we had only a small number. When I was going to that meeting, I had two cases myself. I knew that one of my team had one case. I think my colleague Mr Donnelly had two cases, Mr Liston had one case. So they were scattered around.'

'We had 16 inspectors in the investigation branch. From time to time they would come across a problem not confined necessarily to AIB but to other banks. We were getting a little feel of what was happening, but we had nothing substantial.'

The psychological confrontation worked. Deirdre Fullen, who was taking notes for AIB, left the meeting under the impression that they had got a dressing down from Revenue, and that the whole compliance record of the bank was being called into question.

McCarthy admits it was a fluke. 'During the course of the conversation, whether it was by divine inspiration, by prompting or otherwise I don't know, but it appears that I decided that the compliance of the entire bank situation should be discussed.'

The meeting was important because for the first time he wanted to 'start making noises about the unknown situation of bogus accounts'.

Jimmy O'Mahony admitted straight away that AIB had 'a major problem' in relation to bogus accounts, but he claimed the bank had been working since the previous April to eradicate them from its system. But then he told an untruth, and McCarthy, the wily Revenue man, knew it.

O'Mahony said that AIB had only IR£350 million in non-resident accounts. But McCarthy knew there was about IR£1 billion and he began to wonder where the other IR£650 million had suddenly disappeared to. If it had gone completely out of the banking system the Irish economy would have been affected. But of course, as he would later realise, it hadn't gone anywhere. It was dodgy money or 'funny money' as O'Mahony himself would later describe it. So AIB had simply switched the money from its branch network around the country to its Retail Deposit Centre (RDC), an anonymous office block in Shankhill, south Dublin. It was a technicality to take the money out of its branches where it was becoming noticeable. But the money was still in the bank.

'I knew that was patently untrue,' said McCarthy. 'There was substantial misinformation right at the start.' What puzzled him was why the bank was telling lies.

'I think,' said Don Roddy, another Revenue official present at the meeting, 'that Tony was trying to sort of give the financial institutions, in this case AIB, a rap on the wrist. But he didn't have an awful lot of powers or possibilities of actually getting into the situation in a serious way.'

Trying to explain it nine years later, with the knowledge of what was going on in AIB at the time in those early days of 1991, McCarthy concluded that somehow the top people in the bank thought he was on to them. 'They had an agenda at this stage,' he said. 'They had a little bombshell in their lap, of which I wasn't aware, and they were anxious to get it resolved in their own little way.'

Cleverly, or so it seemed in hindsight, the banker and former taxman Jimmy O'Mahony brought the subject around to 'what if?' What if the banks cleaned up the little mess and did it quickly? Could they rely on the Revenue Commissioners to turn a blind eye to what had gone on in the past?

Now, to use the buzzword they later invented for this purpose, the bank and the Revenue would be 'forward looking' in their approach to the issue of criminality and tax dodging in the bank. After they discussed the 'little bombshell', Jimmy O'Mahony of AIB felt he had come to an arrangement with Tony McCarthy of Revenue.

Indeed, it seemed they had. Because two days later, 15 February 1991, McCarthy wrote to O'Mahony at the bank setting out his view of what was agreed.

'I invited you to have all non-resident accounts re-examined and suggested that each branch manager certify to you that all the accounts in their branch at 10 June 1991 are, insofar as they are aware, genuine non-resident accounts. Any cases discovered prior to 10 June 1991 will be the subject of a DIRT payment to be negotiated at this branch without penalty and without publications. Detection of offences arising after that date will give rise to prosecution of both the bank and the official involved, a point which should be clearly advised to your staff.'

Nine years later, when these events became of vital importance as AIB struggled to wriggle out of the massive tax evasion at the heart of its banking system, this short paragraph became the basis for the amnesty it claimed it had received.

On 26 February, Jimmy O'Mahony of AIB phoned Tony McCarthy in the Investigation Branch. Their conversation was brief 'if it took place at all' according to McCarthy. But O'Mahony, who had taken a note, swore that this constituted the amnesty and that the adoption of a 'forward looking approach' was agreed between him and McCarthy on behalf of the bank and the Revenue.

O'Mahony circulated his interpretation of the meeting and phone call to top executives in AIB, right up to Peter Sutherland, the Chairman, and Gerry Scanlan. They agreed that to carry out McCarthy's wishes they would have to hand over IR£14 million in unpaid DIRT. They nearly took the hand off Revenue to give them the money – knowing already that by their own estimates, as calculated by Anthony Spollen, they owed nearly IR£100 million.

'I telephoned Tony McCarthy in relation to the "amnesty" on non-resident accounts. He views it as an amnesty up to 30 June 1991,' O'Mahony reported back to his AIB bosses. It was an amazing deal. If the bank cleaned up its act and got rid of the thousands of bogus non-resident accounts by re-classifying them as ordinary accounts, then bygones would be bygones and AIB would have no further liability.

O'Mahony was pressed about the vital importance of getting 'something in writing' which AIB could put away in its vaults and rely on in case this matter should ever be raised by Revenue at some future date.

But O'Mahony was reluctant to go back and look for anything official. He knew there was considerable danger in demanding an official amnesty as this would raise serious questions for Revenue, and it might even prompt them to revisit the whole issue and start demanding more information. He answered, 'I can do no more,' and so the top executives in the bank decided to rely on his memo and the note of his phone call.

'In my opinion, the significance of the meeting of 13 February 1991 between officers of the Investigation Branch [Revenue] and AIB personnel on the above matter should be viewed against the background prevailing at the time within the AIB Group,' wrote Tom Tiuit, Principal Inspector of Taxes at the Revenue. 'The intervention by Mr McCarthy was a godsend to the bank in that it afforded an opportunity to the bank to contrive an arrangement which they seek to construe as consent by Revenue to an amnesty in respect of DIRT which ought properly to have been remitted by the bank.'

But there was just one small problem and each day it was getting bigger and bigger. It was the problem of the Internal Auditor. Anthony Spollen was doing his best to screw up the deal, as it might have been put in local parlance.

Unaware at first of the vital meeting with Revenue, Spollen was gradually becoming aware that the bank was claiming an amnesty without having anything in writing from Revenue. He knew it was the beginning of a cover-up and he may well have known that the Revenue and the Central Bank were too weak to really take on AIB. Anthony Spollen's future with AIB was becoming inextricably linked to the convulsions surrounding the DIRT issue. Peter Sutherland, intriguingly, said that there was what he called 'an intermingling' of the transfer of Spollen and the DIRT issue.

On 14 February 1991, Spollen wrote to Brian Wilson, Group General Manager, Ireland: 'The figures now being produced confirm that we have a major problem running into hundreds of million.'

Spollen's solution was that AIB should get together with the other banks, who also had the problem of bogus non-resident accounts, to find a solution. 'It seems to me that a joint approach by the financial institutions to the Revenue with the objective of gaining an amnesty may be the best way of ensuring that the bank does not face a substantial liability at some time in the future,' he said in conclusion to his letter to Brian Wilson.

But, as two senior officials of AIB had negotiated the alleged amnesty for the bank just the day before, this solution was not a runner. Wilson and other senior executives now believed they could get out of the huge liability with a payment of IR£14 million. Why would they want to trouble the Revenue with the exact details of a scam that had been running for years?

Adding to their good fortune, at around the same time 'problems in the drink trade' were identified as more important than tax dodging banks and Tony McCarthy was put in charge of a new investigation.

'I was assigned then to take over Operation Scorpion with a colleague from Cork and another colleague from Dublin, but with substantial other resources available to me as I required them. So I think that would explain the background – whether it was fortunate or unfortunate – to my movement on to the drinks trade,' explained McCarthy.

His files on the biggest scandal in the history of banking were thrown on the floor of his office and there they languished for seven years, gathering dust.

Chapter 10

Spollen Fights Back

As Anthony Spollen, Group Internal Auditor of AIB, leafed through his newspapers on the cold, bitter morning of 28 January 1991, there were few distractions from the stalemate he was facing since being called down to 'HQ' ten days before. He had broken a cardinal rule of the bank; he had said 'no' to the wishes of the Chief Executive.

'The group chief executive of a large institution is not used to being told by people, "I won't go along with you," and I understand that,' he would later recall. But now, sitting in his office in Carrisbrook House, he was separated from the top executives at Bankcentre by about a mile in distance. Unfortunately the gulf that separated him from his bosses was a chasm that could no longer be bridged.

That morning he had read coverage in the papers of the burial the previous day of the former Attorney General, John Kelly, and he had seen among those attending, his Chairman, Peter

Sutherland, a failed Fine Gael politician who had himself occupied that same lofty government position as the witty Mr Kelly, before going into the business of making money in earnest.

Further on, the financial pages informed him that the AIB share price was a steady, but modest, 104p. But despite the apparent solid position of the bank, Spollen, for the first time, put down in writing the evidence of something 'rotten' at the heart of AIB.

Since the 'Dana Affair' Anthony Spollen had felt that maybe he wasn't exactly in the loop about what was going on, that inside information was being kept from him. At the back of his mind now was a memo from Henry O'Brien, an executive in Spollen's department, telling him that there was 'keen anxiety' in Internal Audit about bogus non-resident accounts. This had arisen after a very small sample of the bank's records in Listowel, Co Kerry, found that only three out of fifty forms examined were actually genuine.

These were the famous Form Fs – the declarations signed by customers giving their addresses abroad. If the vast majority in the Listowel branch were bogus, it was not difficult to predict that the same pattern existed throughout the country. The bank knew the accounts were bogus because favoured business customers were using them on a weekly and even on a daily basis to lodge money, much of it untaxed. If a customer was genuinely non-resident they would not be in a position to use the accounts in such a manner.

When the attempt had been made to transfer him, Anthony Spollen had referred to the bank's problem with DIRT and other issues. 'During the period between 18 January and the 22nd or the 23rd there was a discussion about the transfer of Mr Spollen,' Peter Sutherland would later recollect. 'The discussion also involved, between Mr Spollen and some executives, discussions of issues relating to the management and running of the internal audit function and it must have raised the issues of DIRT, of *Octopus* (the Dana Affair) and the other issues that came up subsequently.'

But those issues had been raised verbally as Spollen sought to defend himself from the transfer. Now things were moving on to a more dangerous level.

Anthony Spollen decided to put pen to paper and the correspondence he began that morning would have devastating consequences for AIB. As all good civil servants and executives know, once something is written down it is there on the record and can never be retracted. Some day it will return to haunt you.

Under the heading 'Private and Confidential' he fired off a memo to Brian Wilson, the man who was trying to induce him to 'follow orders' and leave his position as Group Internal Auditor of the bank and come work for him in the 'Ireland Division'. It was friendly, but pointed.

> Non-Resident Deposits
> Dear Brian,
> Don Walsh currently estimates that the size of the Form F problem in the Republic of Ireland could run into hundreds of millions. He has confirmed to me that you and your colleagues are fully aware of

the problem and are considering the situation. Bearing in mind the CRT [Composite Tax Rate] position in Britain, which as you know built up over a number of years and is now costing the bank dearly, you might consider whether or not a large liability is building up in the Ireland division both North and South.

Kind Regards,

Anthony Spollen

The memo was an uncanny precursor of what would later transpire at AIB. But curiously Don Walsh, one of the top inspectors in Internal Audit, would later deny that he ever brought such an estimate to Spollen's attention.

The ball was rolling, all the way into the court of Brian Wilson, the adversary who just over a week earlier had tried to have Spollen moved from his position as Group Internal Auditor.

Two days later, 30 January, Spollen fired off another memo, this time to Don Walsh.

Please quantify immediately the amount of false Form F money on the books of the Group. The estimate (£350-£400 million) which you have given me is frightening.

This whole matter has, I believe, very serious implications for AIB and we must quantify both the potential liability arising from what has taken place to date and ensure that the bank is protected against these type of deposits in the future.

I would like you to confirm to me that our internal audit staff adopt the highest standards in auditing this area and please set out for me what the standards are.

Kind Regards,

Anthony Spollen

Gerry Scanlan, the Chief Executive of AIB, would later claim that he wasn't aware of these exchanges. Indeed, even more amazingly, he would claim that he was not even aware of the level of acrimony that now existed between Spollen, John Keogh and Brian Wilson over the transfer until it was revealed in the *Sunday Independent* seven years after these dramatic events took place.

Having failed to shift Spollen from his job by sending his emissaries Keogh and Walsh, Gerry Scanlan decided on a face-to-face meeting about the abortive transfer. It was arranged for 4 February 1991.

Already warned by Peter Sutherland of the possibility that Anthony Spollen might take legal action against AIB claiming constructive dismissal, it was a tense and difficult meeting between two men who clearly no longer cared very much for each other, personally or professionally.

'I won't put a tooth in it . . . it was a very frank discussion, a full and frank discussion,' said Spollen with his usual discretion. 'Full and frank' is a term used by diplomats to describe a meeting which ends just short of blood on the floor.

At the short and caustic meeting, Gerry Scanlan demanded that Spollen move to his new post. Spollen refused. But then he went further, suggesting that he was being shafted because of his independent stance as Group Internal Auditor. He mentioned the Dana scandal and the resulting cover-up. He made a reference to compliance difficulties with the Bank of England and to the mushrooming problem of bogus non-resident accounts in Ireland. Scanlan replied that this was rubbish.

'You will be moved in 14 days,' he told Spollen, and he gestured for him to leave his office.

Later that day, as he gazed from his fourth-floor suite in the Bankcentre, out over the roofs of south Dublin and the mountains beyond, Gerry Scanlan dictated a note to Anthony Spollen telling him to follow orders in the best quasi-military traditions of the bank. He told Spollen he was appointing him as Chief Manager Corporate Banking at his current grade and salary scale and there would be no further discussion.

> I must confess to have found your suggestion [that Spollen was being moved because of his 'independent stance' about difficult issues] somewhat offensive – that's putting it mildly – but I am prepared to believe that it was made under stress of the moment and that on reflection you will acknowledge that it was unjustified.
>
> 'I am satisfied that there is no element of unfairness or inequity in your transfer, and that it is reasonable in all the circumstances to expect you to

Wicklow County Council
County Library Services

subordinate your personal preferences to your obligations as an AIB executive and to the needs and priorities of AIB as an entity. Accordingly, I formally confirm your appointment to the position of Chief Manager Corporate Banking.

Oddly enough, Scanlan never sent the letter. But he did file it away and years later it would re-surface.

Within hours of the meeting with Scanlan ending, Anthony Spollen was back in his own office talking to his protector Peter Sutherland, keeping him abreast of the latest developments in what was now turning into a financial soap opera. He told the Chairman that Gerry Scanlan was 'less than pleased' about his refusal to accept the transfer and was probably angry because he was 'very conscious that Mr Sutherland and I were very close friends.'

He also repeated to Sutherland the allegations he had made against Scanlan at their face-to-face meeting. For the Chairman of a bank to be informed of such malpractice within his own organisation must have been startling to say the least.

But Sutherland was also getting the other side of the story from Gerry Scanlan, who worked just a short walk down the plush pile carpets on the fourth floor of the bank's head office. Scanlan told Sutherland that he was aware of discussions between Spollen and Sutherland which were happening 'independently' of him.

'Peter Sutherland told me of his concern about Mr Spollen's possibility of taking an action against the bank for wrongful dismissal,' Scanlan remembered.

But as Chief Executive of AIB he was determined to stand firm – friendship was one thing, running a major bank and the single biggest business in Ireland was something entirely different.

'If my writ didn't run throughout the organisation I'd no business there,' he declared, making it clear that, like any good general, he was determined to have his way, despite the friendship between Sutherland and that man he was trying to move.

But Sutherland had bigger concerns. He knew better than anyone else from his own vast legal experience that if an executive bloodbath ended up in a legal tussle in the Four Courts in Dublin, AIB would be the losers, one way or another. Teams of high-priced lawyers and public relations executives would be employed. They would tear various reputations to shreds publicly and privately and Allied Irish Banks' dirty linen would be washed very publicly. Not only would this greatly entertain its competitors and the public at large, but it would warn the Revenue Commissioners of the internal strife about bogus accounts and unpaid DIRT. It would cost the bank dearly, and he was determined to prevent that. After all, that's why he was Chairman of Allied Irish Banks.

As the politician Sean Ardagh said: 'What I am looking at is the overall, I was going to say "rottenness", but the ethos that one would aspire to within a financial institution, particularly the largest financial institution in the State.'

The 'ethos' of the bank was to make money, and clearly that

was Scanlan's main concern. However, Sutherland had his own reputation as well as the long-term reputation of the bank to think about. Sutherland himself was trying other channels to bring peace to his warring executive floor. He phoned James Culliton, Chairman of AIB's Audit Committee and a mutual friend of both Gerry Scanlan and Anthony Spollen.

'I didn't know that Peter Sutherland and Tony Spollen were old schoolmates, I had no idea of that relationship,' said Culliton, who tried his hand at peacemaker and honest broker. But the surprise about the close relationship between Sutherland and Spollen was nothing compared with the shock he got when he was informed of the turn of events now unfolding at the very top levels within the bank. What was being bandied about was that AIB had underestimated its DIRT liability by a fantastic IR£100 million.

'When it came into my domain was when Mr Peter Sutherland phoned me at the end of January or early February and it was in the context of Mr Spollen's allegations that I heard about the transfer. He told me that he had information from the Group Internal Auditor that this [bogus non-resident accounts] was one of a number of very serious allegations he was making about the bank.

> Now I was quite . . . well I was very surprised because on 3 December 1990 we had had our annual review with Mr Spollen and it was an excellent review and there was no question of any underprovision for DIRT – not IR£500,000, not

IR£1 million, not IR£5 million, not any figure.

Mr Sutherland indicated that he was going to raise this with the board and he had in mind setting up a special committee and he would have inquired of me, as Chairman of the Audit Committee, would I be prepared to undertake this special investigation.

But even as Sutherland and Culliton were trying to sort out the mess, Spollen was ploughing ahead with his investigations into the bank's weakest point – the bogus non-resident accounts, the fact that senior executives like John Keogh and Brian Wilson were aware of them and the executive wriggling that was going on over what to tell the taxman.

On 6 February, Brian Wilson replied to Spollen's letters.

Dear Tony,

Thank you for your letter on the subject of Non-Resident Deposits. Don Walsh may have informed you that he and I have already had a number of discussions on this issue. We agreed a programme during 1991 to address the problem, which Don is following up on my behalf and which he will be keeping me informed of progress.

Yours Sincerely,

Brian

In other words – back off.

That same afternoon, after various contacts, Scanlan and Spollen met once again. The meeting started that Tuesday (6 February) at 12.30pm and lasted all of five minutes. Spollen started by telling the Chief Executive that he was receiving disturbing information about the situation in the bank.

But Scanlan halted him.

> I told him he had attributed a motivation to senior executives concerning his transfer. I saw . . . a series of serious allegations. I told him I couldn't accept those allegations on the information available to me. I said to him, 'As we both know, those allegations, if aired in public, could be extremely embarrassing to the bank's reputation. The very process of the bank vindicating itself would also involve embarrassment.'
>
> I said this to Mr Spollen because I had been informed that he was contemplating legal action against the bank for wrongful dismissal – as it was going to be interpreted. I said to Mr Spollen, "I gather you repeated the allegations to Mr Sutherland. In view of the seriousness of your allegations against management, I and other senior colleagues have insisted to the Chairman that they be examined and disposed of." '

Gerry Scanlan told the Internal Auditor that 'on reflection' and in view of the investigation now taking place, it would be 'inappropriate' to proceed with his transfer and he would remain in the position of Group Internal Auditor until 'the situation has been resolved'.

The two men would never speak face-to-face of this issue again, and years later the bitterness between them would still hang like a bad smell when they were both called to account for their behaviour during this explosive period.

'So Mr Spollen's claims against senior management were not sustainable claims?' asked the former detective and Minister for Justice Sean Doherty TD, a member of the committee which eight years later would investigate the whole affair.

'Correct,' replied Mr Scanlan.

'And Mr Spollen was a very aggrieved person, would you believe?'

'I have no difficulty believing it.'

'Are you satisfied that it was impossible to placate Mr Spollen?'

'Well, let me put it to you that there were negotiations going on independently of my involvement with them and that it seems that the only basis on which he was placated ultimately was that he left the bank.'

'He couldn't stay really, would that be correct?' asked Doherty.

'I think it would,' answered Scanlan.

He continued:

> Mr Spollen wrote a letter to Mr Wilson some time
> around 28 January and went off on a significant

new tack, if I might so describe it, and here was something which developed legs to an enormous scale. Now, whether or not that was part of the fallout of the fact that he would not accept the valid instruction from the Chief Executive of the organisation, I don't know.

On 14 February, just a week after his meeting with Scanlan, Spollen returned to the offensive with another letter to Brian Wilson. This time he cleverly brought his other adversary, the man who had tried to have him moved, John Keogh, into the controversy. More importantly, he pinned the bankers down on precisely what was going on between the top brass at AIB and the Revenue Commissioners.

Dear Brian,

John Keogh mentioned to me that Pat O'Mahony (General Manager/Branches AIB) has had unofficial meetings with Revenue people at which he discussed the problem and at which he stated that AIB was getting its house in order.

The figures now being produced confirm that we have a major problem running into hundreds of millions.

Could you please let me have further details of the programme and the initiatives, to address the problem, as mentioned in your letter of February 6.

As part of our audit procedures Group Internal

Audit will now ask Branch Managers to confirm that they understand the directive from yourself and Pat O'Mahony and will also ask them to sign a declaration regarding addresses of non-resident depositors.

How do you propose ensuring that the bank, in Ireland, will not be faced with the same sort of situation to that which has arisen in Britain?

Where do you see the Group's responsibility vis-à-vis the Revenue and the Central Bank on this issue?

It seems to me that a joint approach by the financial institutions to the Revenue with the objective of gaining an amnesty may be the best way of ensuring that the bank does not face a substantial liability at some future date.

Yours,

Tony

As the crisis deepened, Spollen seized on a figure provided to him by AIB's top taxation expert, Jimmy O'Mahony, that 75 per cent of the money in non-resident deposit accounts was hot, untaxed money. By now Spollen had consulted his lawyers and was in discussions with Peter Sutherland about his future in AIB. But like all good legal actions, it was one that would never reach a court of law. It was settled between the two men with the utmost discretion. In the end, Anthony Spollen would receive what one insider described as 'an offer he couldn't refuse'.

Perhaps he got it after his letter to Brian Wilson, dated 6 March 1991, which was a damning indictment of the bank and would be catastrophic for any financial institutions less robust than AIB was at the time.

Under the heading 'Bogus Non-Resident Deposits', it read:

Dear Brian,

For the purposes of calculating the DIRT which should have been deducted in the half year to October, 1990, Jimmy O'Mahony and the financial control people have assumed that 60 per cent of all accounts designated non-resident are bogus: on this basis the figure is close to £10 million.

The number of bogus non-resident accounts involved is estimated to be in the region of 53,000 and of these 17,000 approximately have no forms and 36,000 have forms but are bogus – clearly a very serious problem.

Jimmy O'Mahony states that we cannot get confirmation that an amnesty is being offered as this would require legislation which he feels is not desirable for this type of issue.

We cannot therefore say that we do not have a huge potential liability . . . If we calculate the DIRT for the year 31/3/91 on these bogus accounts as being close to £20 million . . . and if the problem has been improving significantly over the past years as was indicated to the Investigation Branch, it does not need me to say to you that the potential liability is very large indeed.

It is not clear from the letter if the DIRT payment to be negotiated with the Investigation Branch is for one year or more than that.

Yours,

Tony

The following day Wilson wrote back to say, 'I understand that John Keogh has arranged a meeting on these matters with the Central Bank, though I would be very surprised if they were not well up to date on what is, after all, a long standing and industry wide issue.'

The day after that Spollen was in even better fighting form:

Dear Brian,

Your letter of March 7 refers to my estimates – these are the estimates of Jimmy O'Mahony and the financial control people (which was spelt out quite clearly in my letter to you on March 6) and the sheer scale is staggering; to have 53,000 bogus non-resident accounts with a value close to £600 million is a shocking situation. I wonder were these the figures which Mr O'Mahony had in mind when conveying to the Revenue the determined effort which was made to ensure that all non-resident accounts as at April 1990 were genuine.

I don't want to go over the points made in my

letter of March 6 to you, but it is very unclear as to what the bank's potential liability is – ignoring previous years, the estimate, for the DIRT which should have been deducted from these bogus accounts in October, 1990 is close to £10 million – whether the bank must provide for this in the accounts to March 1991 needs to be quickly clarified. (I mentioned this to John Keogh prior to last Tuesday's board meeting – at the Audit Committee that afternoon the matter wasn't mentioned – perhaps it was at the board.)

Your contention that the Central Bank is well up to date on the issue is interesting . . . you might let me know of the evidence which you have to support this. Are you saying that the Central Bank is turning a blind eye to a matter which is costing the government a fortune in lost revenue?

Yours,

Tony

PS Jimmy O'Mahony has just informed me that he has had no discussions with the Revenue regarding the £10 million referred to in paragraph 2.

Spollen now knew that the bank hadn't and couldn't get a written amnesty from the Revenue Commissioners, and he suspected that the supposed discussion with the Central Bank was a bluff.

In fact, it wasn't a bluff but the Central Bank was in such awe of AIB that it wouldn't matter. They didn't believe wholesale tax evasion by one of the banks they were supposed to regulate had anything at all to do with them.

Spollen was causing Wilson a lot of angst and along the way he was dragging Scanlan and John Keogh into the frame.

Anthony Spollen was certainly not going to go quietly. Before he left, the air was blue with memos and reports to other executives, reports and counter reports to the board of AIB and numerous discussions with his friend Peter Sutherland who would play a pivotal role in sorting out the whole sorry mess.

But more importantly for AIB, Sutherland would play the Chairman's role brilliantly, even if some of his underlings would later refer to the episode as 'sealing in the smell'.

And IR£100 million left a powerful smell in the cash-strapped Ireland of 1991.

Chapter 11

Crisis on the Fourth Floor

Unknown to the Revenue Commissioners, who had suspicions
but no hard evidence of what was going on in AIB, the bank itself
was consumed by the issue of DIRT and bogus non-resident
accounts.

As the drama began to unfold, some of Anthony Spollen's staff
believed they knew exactly who was controlling the crisis –
Spollen himself. At the end of January and the beginning of
February 1991, as the 'private and confidential' memos began to
criss-cross each other in the internal mail system, Spollen gave
the clear impression that somehow these figures had been
produced to him from a variety of other executives. But Don
Walsh, Head of Internal Audit Ireland, believed that Spollen had
seized on the issue which left the bank most vulnerable and was
turning it into a giant internal crisis that would grab the attention
of the board and the Chairman of the bank.

Since Gerry Scanlan had attempted to move Spollen, Allied

Irish Banks had moved into the throes of a major power struggle, with Scanlan and his lieutenants ranged on one side and Anthony Spollen alone on the other. Well, not quite all alone, he did have the ear of the Chairman through a friendship that went back more than thirty years. In terms of a power struggle, he was actually orchestrating the series of events now unfolding. His revenge was sweet and it was ruthless.

But the truth was that Anthony Spollen, while a loyal company man, was probably too straight for his own good. In a large ambitious organisation like AIB, the ruthless nature of international high finance meant that risks were taken; the government was effectively bullied and, unless you marched to the military ethos of following orders, you were going to get left behind.

Spollen knew there was something seriously illegal about the bank's position on bogus accounts and on 28 January 1991, the same day that AIB believed they were inching towards a deal with Revenue, he suddenly raised the issue with Walsh. Two days later he wrote again saying the estimate of IR£400 million (contained in bogus accounts), which he alleged Walsh had given him, was 'frightening'. Of course the estimate was right, the only problem was that Don Walsh claims he never gave him such a figure.

'There is no way that I raised this as a problem issue with Mr Spollen in January 1991,' said Walsh later. He had carried out an exercise in Northern Ireland eight months previously which had produced some disturbing figures, but not the ones Spollen was suddenly plucking from the air with such accuracy.

It must also be kept in mind that Jim Culliton had told Spollen to put everything in writing because events were moving beyond the executive floor and up to the boardroom where the very important people who ran the bank would have to decide what (or who) was right and what (or who) was wrong. Spollen, like the clever banker he was, did just that, knowing that in all likelihood the crisis would result in blood being spilt on the floor of the boardroom of Allied Irish Banks.

When Walsh couldn't, or wouldn't, come up with the figures to back up Spollen's position, there was some uncharacteristic behaviour on the part of the Group Internal Auditor.

'At that point Mr Spollen went physically straight past me to the technology audit people and asked them to undertake this exercise which suggested to me, I have to say, at the time that Mr Spollen had pre-decided on this course of action to go to the technology audit section. And it conveyed to me that he seemed to be very, very determined to come up with the figures,' said Walsh. 'Certainly those letters, I would say, did put a strain on our working relationship around about that time.'

Spollen's general demeanour, according to his underlings became a little more unpredictable. But Walsh wasn't the only one perturbed. Jimmy O'Mahony, the man on whose brief and unrecorded phone call with Revenue led AIB to depend on a tax amnesty, was also mystified as to how, just when he believed he had carried off the 'deal of his career' with Revenue, there seemed to be a determined effort by the Internal Auditor to undermine his position.

O'Mahony stated,

> Mr Spollen has attributed to me the basis of the
> estimate of 53,000 bogus non-resident accounts
> with balances of IR£600 million which he included
> in his report. I have to say emphatically that I would
> not have had any way of knowing the precise extent
> or even the basis of an accurate estimate of bogus
> non-resident accounts in existence at that time. I
> stated last year that I had no recollection of the 60
> per cent estimate, but if I did use that figure it
> would only have been a 'guesstimate'. I now
> understand that some estimates were made at a
> meeting at which I was present where the possible
> effects of reclassifying accounts were being looked
> at and the 60 per cent estimate was used there, but
> again as a 'guesstimate'.

So, if Don Walsh and Jimmy O'Mahony were not giving him the
information but Spollen was attributing it to them, what on earth
was going on? Of course, Walsh, and to a lesser extent
O'Mahony, didn't fully realise that they were merely pawns in a
much bigger game – a power struggle at the very top of the bank.

As things began to unfold in the early weeks of February 1991,
James Culliton, one of the country's must successful corporate
figures and Chairman of AIB's powerful Audit Committee, could
only look on in increasing bewilderment. Later he said:

> Oh, like we weren't innocents abroad in that we sat

there on 3 December 1990 and we had no notion of problems in the bank about DIRT. Please get me right on this one. It was an ongoing problem and had been for a long time, but it wasn't brought to our notice as an audit committee that it was in any way a serious problem which would have required a level of extra provision for taxation, not at that stage.

Culliton, who had been the head of CRH, one of Ireland's largest corporations, knew a bit about offshore banking through his own Ansbacher account and was a very careful man. As Chairman of the Audit Committee of Allied Irish Bank it was his job to guard against such problems suddenly appearing. Now, although he had only been vaguely aware of a minor problem prior to this, the bank was, according to the Group Internal Auditor, facing a IR£100 million liability.

As the letters went to and fro, Culliton had become increasingly alarmed.

When Anthony Spollen met the powerful Audit Committe of Sir Peter Froggatt, Sir Douglas Morpeth, Dr Liam St John Devlin, Professor Seamus Sheehy, Denis J Murphy and Gerry Scanlan on 3 December 1990, he had given them a 'comprehensive report' and they had patted him on the back, well apart from Scanlan that is, and told him what a good job he was doing. And there hadn't been any mention of DIRT or bogus non-resident accounts.

Now, less than three months later, with the Annual General

Meeting of the bank looming, there was a liability of IR£100 million on the table. Culliton concluded:

> Well I can assure you, we didn't regard the £100 million as a fiction. In fact, as a committee, we began to wonder was there some sort of conspiracy going on that didn't include us. These were the sort of thoughts that come up into your mind when you see £100 million put down. But I think what happened between 6 January, when we met as a board, and the end of January was a very difficult industrial relations dispute.

An industrial relations dispute involving the Chief Executive and the Group Internal Auditor? Hardly the normal term to use for a corporate power struggle, but apt perhaps for what was really happening.

Perhaps Gerry Scanlan had a more succinct way of putting it: 'I have long since concluded that the £100 million is a total fiction.'

But fact or fiction, it so deeply troubled Chairman Peter Sutherland, who was caught in a difficult position between the bank's executives on the one hand and his friendship with Spollen on the other, that he had to do something:

> Well, I can only imagine what my reaction was rather than have a specific recollection of it. I was obviously very concerned about the serious nature

Wicklow County Council
County Library Services

of the various issues that were being raised. I had more or less, through the process, contact with the other board members who were involved in the audit sub-committee that was looking into the issue, but I did not intervene in any way. It wasn't appropriate for me to do so. It was a question of that process being brought to a conclusion. I would also have heard and know of the executive response which, of course, was in disagreement.

Whatever does he mean? 'I knew exactly what was going on but I didn't want to get involved.' But he was involved, whether he liked it or not. He continued:

We were in the course of dealing with an issue which had been orally expressed and on which there was clearly a disagreement and we felt that the best way to proceed with this was to set up a sub-committee and to ask those concerned, particularly the Internal Auditor, to set out in writing any issues or complaints which he had in order that we could deal with them in a manner which was appropriate. I can't think of any way that would be appropriate to deal with this matter other than the way that we did deal with it and I am frankly rather proud of the fact that this process was done with the objectivity that it was done with.

It was now over to the Audit Committe of AIB to decide what course of action it must take. Should it bury the scandal? Or should it, as Spollen had advised, go the Revenue, the Central Bank and the Department of Finance, and admit that it had systematically defrauded the state of IR£100 million in unpaid taxes? Jimmy Culliton tried to explain how they came to their decision:

> We were the independent five or six just men. We were the ones charged with sorting this out and what we did was, I think as any jury is required to do, hear as much evidence, relevant evidence, as you can get and then weigh it up and decide on the balance of the evidence that you have. And that was our approach. I'm quite satisfied that Tony Spollen was given every opportunity to present his case in writing and verbally and, I have to say, that John Keogh's rebuttal, in his letter of 25 March, was hugely significant.

What John Keogh told the bank's most senior directors was startling but very comforting. 'I am advised by our group taxation department, Dr de Buitléir and Mr [Jimmy] O'Mahony, both former officials of the Irish Revenue, with Dr de Buitléir being a very senior official, that all financial institutions have, in effect, an amnesty for the past, provided we fully regularise the position by 30 June 1991.'

Pat O'Mahony, who was in charge of AIB's branch network

around Ireland, explained that before February 1991 they were making an effort to clean the bogus non-resident accounts out of the system, but certainly after the 'deal' they became far more rigorous in their attitude, to the point of threatening to fire bank managers who were found to have bogus accounts on their books.

In essence, the board of AIB, and particularly Peter Sutherland, was faced with a dilemma. They had to choose between their Group Internal Auditor, who was telling them they had a liability of IR£100 million to the Irish State, or the Group Finance Director, John Keogh, who was telling them they had an amnesty. But mostly they believed the whole crisis was one that could easily have been avoided altogether.

For the board it was purely a matter of business. But Peter Sutherland was being asked to choose between the interests of the bank and a lifelong friendship.

Chapter 12

The Board Decides

As he gazed over the carnage that was engulfing him, businessman and Chairman of the Audit Committee of AIB James Culliton could only shake his head in wonderment. He would later describe the way he felt as events unfolded before him as 'absolutely flabbergasted'. It was no mean admission for a man who had seen most things in a long and distinguished career in Irish business.

'How did the liability rocket from nil to IR£100 million in about eight weeks, that was what made us sceptical about the IR£100 million, not about Mr Spollen or not about his judgement in terms of the way he perceived it, but like how could it become IR£100 million from nothing eight weeks earlier?' Culliton mused.

It was also a matter of some concern to the board of Allied Irish Banks. First, they had a bloodbath at executive level and second, they were facing a huge potential liability if Spollen's dire predictions proved true. In terms of share price, AIB was still behind Bank of Ireland but it was gradually overtaking its more 'establishment' and cautious rival.

But it had to be careful. In 1989 AIB's profits were IR£155 million and in 1990 they were IR£237 million, but in 1991, as the government tightened its belt and as the bank began to reclassify accounts and lose some of the 'hot money' it had nurtured, profits fell back to IR£178 million and confidence was dented in the process. But these were secondary matters. The real crisis was on the fourth floor of the Bankcentre.

When the board of AIB met on 6 February 1991, Peter Sutherland was authorised to set up a special committee to investigate Spollen's allegations and Sutherland decided that the bank's Audit Committee should do the job.

'I was at a bit of a loss to know how to field these, because they were huge allegations,' said Jim Culliton, who was the Chairman of the committee that would hear both sides and then go to the full board of the bank with a report. He was closely advised by the company's Law Officer, Brian Sheridan, on how he should proceed.

There were allegations and counter allegations, and there was the threat of legal action by Spollen, who also happened to be a personal friend of the Chairman of the bank. It was not an easy task for Culliton to undertake.

'Our law officer told us you always have to have regard for natural justice. He [Sheridan] said, "There's an individual concerned here, Mr Spollen, and he, you know, is very serious about the allegations he's making. So you're going to need a series of meetings and you're going to need to play it in a legal framework." So I explained to Mr Spollen what we were going to do and I said, "Please will you write everything down."'

Culliton sought a written report from Anthony Spollen which he then gave to the Financial Director, John Keogh. He was asked to give a written defence of his position and both men were then called for lengthy interviews by the Audit Committee.

When he convened a meeting of the Audit Committee of Allied Irish Banks on the instructions of the Chairman on 11 March 1991, Culliton already knew from his discussions with Peter Sutherland that there was something seriously wrong in the upper echelons of the bank. The special session was convened to discuss the reports of both men, interview them individually and consider what should be done next.

Dated the day before the meeting, the allegations that were made by the Group Internal Auditor, Anthony Spollen, were a damning indictment of AIB and could not be taken lightly. The bank stood accused of robbing its own Widows and Orphans pension fund, of defrauding the British taxpayer, of issuing a cheque for IR£26 million belonging to beef baron Larry Goodman without the proper authorisation and a litany of other serious malpractices.

Oddly enough, it was only at item number three in his long litany of wrongdoings that Spollen came to the huge, IR£100 million DIRT scandal that the bank and its customers were perpetrating against the Irish State through the use of bogus non-resident accounts. But probably most of his ire was reserved for the attempt by the top management of the bank to downgrade the function of Internal Audit, a job that Spollen and his 80-strong staff took very seriously.

His report read:

> The matters set out in this memorandum have caused great concern to the Internal Audit department of the group and various efforts have been made to bring the specific problems referred to, to the attention of the Chief Executive, Mr Scanlan, and Mr Keogh. The matters are considered serious and relevant to the group and require a specific report to the Audit Committee if Internal Audit is to fulfil their 'mission' as outlined in the group policy document.
>
> Over the past twelve months a number of issues outlined in this memorandum have been brought to the attention of the Chief Executive, John Keogh and other senior authorities within the group. Emphasis of the problem has resulted in pressure being brought to bear on the personnel resources within this department, in particular, efforts to remove and/or transfer the Department and Functionary Head. It has been suggested that the approach taken by the department is too conservative and fails to ignore 'commercial reality'.
>
> Such an attitude may in the short term benefit the bank but over the long term the writer believes it will cause difficulties. It certainly does not reflect a

true and fair view of the assets and liabilities of the group at this point in time.

There are serious problems within the group as outlined herein which need attention and the group must be shown at least to be trying to deal with the problems and reflect the problems in their accounts in a correct and proper manner, taking into account current practises in western economies. Failure to address the issues will result in penalties being imposed by authorities and/or, the department believes, criminal or civil prosecution of bank employees and bank officers including possible prosecution of its directors.

In addition, the reputation, prestige and image of the group will be severely damaged, thereby undermining its assets and long term share values, rendering it vulnerable to outside competing interests.

The issues that need immediate attention are as follows:-

1. *Octopus*. [The share placing for Dana Petroleum already referred to.]

2. The British tax problem. [Failure to deal with bogus non-resident accounts in Britain which had already resulted in substantial penalties being levied against the bank by the tax authorities there.] Because of the recent

developments with the investigation branch [of the] Revenue Commissioners, Republic of Ireland . . . they should be appraised immediately of the British tax situation as ultimately the accounts of the group will have to explain the substantial payment.

3. Non-resident accounts in the Republic of Ireland. This can be described as what is euphemistically called in the Republic of Ireland the Form F problem. As the committee no doubt are aware, there are substantial sums deposited with the group in the Republic of Ireland. The depositors hold themselves out as being non-resident and, in conjunction with bank officers, accounts are opening up wherein the account holders are held out as being non-residents. These are in fact bogus accounts and estimates of the bank indicate that at least 60 per cent of non-resident accounts are bogus. The absence of any documentation for a large number of accounts has been the subject of comment and report in many Internal Audit reports.

This problem, we believe, is now reaching critical proportions particularly since the problem at '2' referred to has emerged and due to the close level of liaison between Her Majesty's Revenue Service and the Revenue

Commissioners in the Republic of Ireland. The exposure of the group is substantial both in financial terms and in respect of the current tax laws. The problem is, in the opinion of this department, now becoming acute since communications emanated from the Investigation Branch of the Office of the Chief Inspector of Taxes on 15 February 1991 and it emerged that the Group Taxation department confirmed that a determined effort was made to ensure that by April 1990 all non-resident accounts, in so far as it could be ascertained, belonged to non-residents. This is clearly not the case.

Non-resident accounts in the Republic of Ireland must be looked at and the problem must be resolved. The committee that has been put in place by the Ireland Division has a huge task ahead of it. Internal Audit are concerned at the contents of the letter of 15 February 1991, from DA McCarthaigh, Office of the Chief Inspector of Taxes, to James O'Mahony, Group Taxation Manager. In this letter the Revenue make a number of points which concern the group, in particular the following:

It is suggested that a determined effort was made to eliminate non-resident accounts by April 1990. This is clearly not the case.

The Revenue suggests that a sample core of non-resident accounts be examined and that 'unusual or unexpected preponderance' be notified to the bank. Furthermore it is suggested that they be investigated by this department. This is of serious significance for the bank in that it is already known without close examination that at least 60 per cent of the accounts are bogus.

The arrangement that has been reached would suggest that a failure to report detection of offences would give rise to prosecution of the bank, presumably the officers and directors and/or the officials involved. Since the Revenue Commissioners appear to be relying on this department, it imposes a serious responsibility on this department to protect the personnel resources of the group and the bank officers.

The Revenue will rely on the bank to impose penalties on its officers who prove themselves 'wayward'. If the bank fails to do this the Irish Revenue will assess the bank's 'earnestness' from its efforts.

The Revenue suggests all non-resident accounts should be re-examined by 30 June 1991. They also suggest that any DIRT tax be paid. This would appear to impose on the bank a responsibility to pay the DIRT although the Revenue suggest that no interest or penalty will be due and no publication will be made of the payment. The letter and communication does not indicate the period of time applicable.

The letter clearly states that detection of offences arising after 30 June 1991 will give rise to prosecution of the bank and its officials involved. This is unequivocal and clear and could, in addition, result in difficulties with the regulatory bodies including the Central Bank. This Irish tax problem is now nearing a critical stage as is borne out by the communications from the Revenue Commissioners. It is a problem that must be addressed by the group and proper provision must be made for the 'DIRT payments' referred to in the letter of 15 February 1991.

4. ABP Holdings. [Relates to problems with a IR£22.8 million cheque belonging to the Goodman Group and Larry Goodman, which was transferred with 'inappropriate or incorrect mandates'.]

5. Micro-Vision. [Relates to huge losses in a British investment.]

6. NEXT Bonds. [An IR£80 million valuation by the bank of bonds just three months before, now had a value of just IR£7 million.]

7. Unwarranted interference with Internal Audit. All of the above problems and difficulties have been brought to the attention of the Chief Executive by way of a direct report or through normal channels, namely John Keogh.

They pose serious problems and difficulties for the group and they are problems which must be addressed now. A failure to address the problems will result in long-term losses to the group. It is accepted that this department may adopt a conservative view to the problems addressed but, by the same token, the problems cannot be ignored and some firm policy must be adopted to protect officers, directors and other interested parties.

In the course of discussions with the Chief Executive, the Chief Executive has suggested that if these issues are raised outside the group it will cause the bank great damage. If the bank does not address the problems now, in the long term this damage will be suffered as the problems, particularly the problem with the Irish Revenue Commissioners, is now nearing a critical crisis point.

Emphasis of the problems herein and requests to deal with them have resulted in counter-productive pressures being brought to bear on this department. In particular, in January steps were taken to move and/or transfer or downgrade the Group Internal Auditor by the Chief Executive.

The motivation must be critically examined by the Audit Committee as must the various issues referred to, namely items 1–7. The position that prevails wherein Internal Audit reports to the Chief Executive can give rise to a situation wherein conflict arises. The Chief Executive, as the party responsible for the performance of the bank, its profits, margins, its loss ratio, its share value, has an understandable interest in promoting this aspect of bank policy. By the same token, it provides an incentive to downgrade Internal Audit and/or choose to ignore warnings that emanate from this department.

The current reporting structure must be examined so that conflict does not arise and the bank or group is afforded maximum protection as are its officers, directors, investors and shareholders and the group is shown to meet its obligations to regulatory bodies and outside authorities.

Signed

Anthony Spollen

Group Internal Auditor

As Spollen was making his submission, the atmosphere was not the usual cold, sterile one typically associated with boardroom investigations.

'Mr Spollen was deeply upset. Deeply, deeply upset and I could understand it and at times it was quite emotional,' remembered Jim Culliton. 'That doesn't in any way take from the way we perceived him to be. He was still the same excellent person and excellent head of the function he was in December or earlier, but that was the ingredient that had come in and we had to cope with that.'

When it came to Keogh's rebuttal of these accusations, the main thrust of his argument was that it was his department who brought the problem of bogus non-resident accounts to the attention of the Internal Auditor, not the other way round. Keogh attempted to forensically demolish Spollen's case in his report, also dated 10 March 1991.

'I am not aware, nor are my colleagues, of any instance where Mr Spollen was prevented from making a specific report to the Audit Committee,' he declared.

He claimed that Spollen had discussed leaving his post with Roy Douglas, Group General Manager, Britain, and had discussed the feasibility of the move with his wife, who had agreed to it.

On the Dana Affair, Keogh said, 'The matter was reported to the AIB board on 5 December 1989 after first being submitted to Sutherland and Scanlan. 'The Keogh Report' was accepted by the board. Therefore, in terms of what should or should not have been done, the issue is closed.'

He then proceeded to the problem of bogus non-resident accounts. He claimed that this was an industry-wide issue and that the financial institutions had an amnesty, as negotiated by the two former Revenue officials who now headed the AIB tax department.

'The whole issue is very much a continuing one. It is obvious from the papers circulated by Mr Spollen that the management of Ireland Division is dealing with it in a committed and structured way. We have an excellent working relationship with the Irish Revenue who are appreciative of our efforts.'

Keogh's response concluded on a harsher note, however:

'Unless there is found to be substance to the claims made by the Group Internal Auditor in respect of the above issues, then the allegations of interference must collapse. It is respectfully suggested that the members of the Audit Committee will find no substance to the above claims and, accordingly, that they will reject the allegations of unwarranted interference with, and improper pressure on, Group Internal Audit. If the members of the Committee do so find, then it follows that they should give serious consideration to the judgement of the Group Internal Auditor in his approach and conduct in relation to these matters.'

The Audit Committee of AIB met on five different occasions up to May 6 to discuss and tease out the implications of Spollen's report and Keogh's reply. Each time the minutes noted 'apologies for inability to attend were conveyed on behalf of the bank's Chief Executive Gerald B Scanlan'. He had, said Jim Culliton, decided to 'opt out'.

'There was a huge conflict of evidence,' said Culliton, after considering the submissions and cross-examinations of both men. 'We were making recommendations based on our investigations. We were not deciding any issue. Our job was to investigate the allegations and to assemble all the information we could and we put that before the board, not just in a slim document but in quite a voluminous one as well that accompanied it. And it was for the board as a whole to determine the issues and what to do about them.'

The final report was signed off by the heavyweight committee of Culliton, Liam St John Devlin, Sir Peter Froggatt, Sir Douglas Morpeth, Denis J Murphy and Seamus J Sheehy on 6 May.

For 'better or worse' they believed that a deal was done with the Revenue Comissioners and that it was well documented by the senior officials in their tax department. Relying on this and swayed by the persuasive arguments of John Keogh, their report, to be presented to the full board of the bank, found that each of the issues raised by Spollen was 'receiving full and proper attention within the group'. In other words, these worthy and 'just' men found comfort in Keogh's version of events and a convenient excuse for the bank to do nothing.

When the full board of AIB met on 27 May, it acknowledged Spollen's assessment that AIB could owe the Revenue Commissioners more than IR£100 million but accepted Keogh's contention that this did not arise because they had an amnesty with the Revenue Commissioners.

'I was happy, rightly or wrongly, to accept the meeting,' said Peter Sutherland. 'I was happy to accept the view of the most notable expert that I know to this day on revenue matters,

Dr de Butléir, and the tax department. His view, I think, is one which I still view with great respect.'

Others were overjoyed. Gerry Scanlan and his top lieutenants, John Keogh and Brian Wilson, had been vindicated.

'At that point, for me at least, the debate on these things was somewhat academic because, as I understood it, we'd reached an agreement with the Revenue and my priority in the Ireland Division was to get the system compliant in time by those dates and, in other words, estimates didn't matter, what mattered was doing the whole exercise through every branch and every case,' said Brian Wilson, Group General Manager, Ireland.

The board of AIB had the added comfort of assurances from Jimmy 'The Pheasant' O'Mahony that he had achieved an amnesty through his meeting, letters and phone call with Tony McCarthy of the Revenue Commissioners. The only difficulty for him and the bank was that there was nothing in writing. But that was another day's work and if everybody was walking away from the issue, then there was nothing to worry about.

'Mr McCarthy is an unlikely Santa Clause, isn't he?' he was asked.

'Well he was a tough negotiator, but honourable,' answered O'Mahony. He then went one better. He said that McCarthy told him on several occasions that he was 'acting with the authority of the board of the Revenue Commissioners'.

When there was a query about who knew of the amnesty, he replied: 'Well up to the board of the Revenue Commissioners as far as I was concerned because he [McCarthy] was telling us he was acting with the approval of the board and that happened on more than one occasion.'

Now all that needed to be done, to use the words of one senior executive, was to 'seal in the smell'.

Anthony Spollen had successfully beaten his Chief Executive in the 'transfer battle' but he had lost the war and now there was nowhere for him to go. He had alienated the top management, he had been rebuffed by the Audit Committee, he had been snubbed by the full board of Allied Irish Banks. The only friend he had left was Peter Sutherland and even he had greater interests than friendship to safeguard.

'The whole issue in relation to this matter [DIRT] and Mr Spollen were directly intertwined; the issues were inextricably mixed,' Sutherland would later declare. 'When the discussion that took place at the end of January in regard to Mr Spollen's position became the focal point for a lot of discussion internally, which it did over a comparatively short period, it was linked with a number of issues which he believed to be of considerable importance and which he believed, as indicated in his memorandum of 10 March, had to be addressed urgently and were of serious concern to him.' Sutherland was a consummate professional at saying very little, but taking a long time to say it.

Now Anthony Spollen had two choices: quit and become a 'whistleblower' in the true sense of the word, or negotiate his way out of AIB. But Anthony Spollen was, if anything, a loyal company man and that's the way he would stay even though he knew his fate was sealed.

He only had to look around him to see that the upheaval that he had caused was already beginning to have a dramatic effect on

AIB Internal Auditor Anthony Spollen, the man who discovered 53,000 bogus accounts in the bank containing IR£600 million, about to enter the DIRT hearings in Dublin.

'God's Banker': Peter Sutherland, Chairman of AIB in 1991. All his
diplomatic skills were needed to keep the DIRT scandal top secret.

Gerald B Scanlan, Chief Executive of AIB – his clash with Spollen led to an executive battle at the Bankcentre in Ballsbridge, Dublin 4.

James Livingstone, head of the Special Inquiry Branch
of the Revenue Commissioners. The murder of his wife Grace, in
Malahide, Co Dublin has never been solved.

Charles J Haughey with the 'bagman' James Desmond
(Des) Traynor – the man behind the offshore
Guinness Mahon Cayman Trust.

Businessman and former rugby international Ray McLoughlin,
author of 'A Note to John Furze'.

AIB's tax experts Deirdre Fullen and Jimmy O'Mahony who laid the foundation for AIB's 'amnesty' with the Revenue Commissioners.

Former AIB Chairman Jim Culliton, who resigned his directorships after his Ansbacher account was revealed. Culliton was described by the Chairman of the DIRT Inquiry, Jim Mitchell, as a 'truthful witness'.

Lochlann Quinn, Chairman of AIB who discovered the bank's darkest secret when he read the *Sunday Independent* on April 5th 1998.

Dermot Gleeson, ex-Attorney General, represented AIB at the DIRT hearings and is now Chairman of the bank.

Taking the oath at the DIRT hearings (L to R): Anthony Spollen former Internal Auditor AIB, Philip Brennan, head of Group Taxation AIB and Brian Wilson, General Manager for Ireland, AIB.

The DIRT Committee (L to R): Bernard Durkan TD, Jim Mitchell TD Chairman, Pat Rabbitte TD, Sean Doherty TD, Denis Foley TD and Sean Ardagh TD.

Margaret Walsh of accountancy firm PWC. She thought AIB had a
second 'amnesty' with the Revenue Commissioners.

Jim Mitchell TD presided over the historic DIRT Inquiry.

John Bruton, now the EU Ambassador to the United States.
As Minister for Finance he made the banks responsible for
collecting the DIRT tax in his 1996 Budget.

Mark Healy Hutchinson, the patrician Chief Executive of
Bank of Ireland.

the executive floor of Allied Irish Banks. On 31 May he attended the leaving party of his one-time friend, John Keogh, the man who had tried to implement Scanlan's order to transfer him. The two had hardly spoken since, so it was surreal for Keogh when he saw Anthony Spollen arriving at the function to wish him well in the future. 'Well, I thought it was strange in the circumstances I suppose, yeah,' he said later when asked about the event.

But it wouldn't be long before Anthony Spollen himself would be having his own retirement party. Having presided over the official whitewash, his school friend Peter Sutherland was now left to pick up the pieces and smooth Spollen's exit from the bank. But more importantly, he had to do it with stealth so that not a whisper of the rift or the bank's huge tax liability would ever seep from the secret files buried in the vaults of AIB, deep in the heart of Dublin 4.

Chapter 13

Sealing in the Smell

When the ICI debacle happened to AIB back in 1985, the bank adopted a professional approach to the crisis that was unprecedented for the country at that particular time. Secrecy was the first priority.

Nobody was to know about the crisis that could bring down the bank until the bank was ready. Then the crisis was to be carefully stage managed so that at all times the Chairman of AIB and his top executives were in total control of the situation. It required secrecy and iron discipline.

Through an ultra-discreet public relations firm in Dublin, Allied Irish Banks' Chief Executive Gerry Scanlan made contact with a group of American experts who were flown into Dublin with the express purpose of advising the board and senior management of AIB on their 'exit' strategy from the insurance company which was threatening to bring down the entire bank. Over a number of days of crisis discussions they carefully considered a number of options, but in the end there was one defined strategy – to panic the Irish government and the then Taoiseach, himself an economist, Dr Garret FitzGerald, into taking the problem off their hands.

It worked like a charm.

They selected a Friday evening to reveal the crisis, and it was no ordinary Friday. It was the Friday of the St Patrick's Day weekend. They manipulated the politicians perfectly. The State radio and television service had virtually closed down for the holiday so the public was kept largely ignorant of what was going on.

In a succession of short sharp shocks, the government was persuaded that ICI's mounting losses would not only bring down Allied Irish Banks itself, but it could quite easily bring down the entire banking system of the State. The government agreed to buy the loss-making insurance company from Allied Irish Banks for IR£1 and to take on its future liabilities, which at the time could have run into hundreds of millions of pounds as a result of reckless gambling on the London 'futures' market. Then AIB went on to make record profits and pay out a higher dividend than ever before to its grateful shareholders.

Now, just six years later, Allied Irish Banks was in the throes of yet another crisis. Suspecting that the Revenue Commissioners were nosing around the issue of bogus non-resident accounts and informed by its Group Internal Auditor, Anthony Spollen, that it might have a liability of IR£100 million, there was once again the imperative of a carefully thought-out strategy and the utmost secrecy. Who better to entrust which such a task but Peter

Sutherland, the politician, lawyer and Chairman of AIB? Peter Sutherland had the added advantage of being extremely close to Anthony Spollen and knew that ultimately, despite the cantankerous letters and the scathing report to the board, he was, at heart, a company man.

But the departure of such an eminent figure as the Group Internal Auditor in a large bank had to be treated with the utmost discretion and delicacy so that none of the questions he was raising within the bank about its liability for unpaid taxes would ever surface publicly.

'Over the years in the job and when I left the bank I kept my counsel,' said Anthony Spollen later, a sad look creasing his soft features. 'I didn't speak to anybody in terms of the matter. My great friend Niall Crowley . . . he never knew why I left AIB. He was my great friend, my mentor. All my oldest friends often wondered . . . and when I saw my package being printed in the newspaper, my severance package [from AIB], and my kids saying, "What's all this about?" That wasn't easy.'

None of it was easy for Anthony Spollen in those upheavals during the early months of 1991. He had gone head to head with Gerry Scanlan and managed to defy the Chief Executive, a dictatorial figure who was used to getting his own way, a man who knew that he couldn't afford to be thwarted if he wanted to retain control of such a large ambitious organisation. He found himself pitted against two senior colleagues, Keogh and Wilson, one of them at least, John Keogh, being a long-standing friend.

Anthony Spollen had done the right thing. He had emphasised at board level that the situation with bogus non-resident accounts was a major problem within the bank and the way they were dealing it would, one day, come back to haunt them. He had the foresight to know that the verbal amnesty that AIB claimed to have with the Revenue Commissioners would not stand up to official scrutiny.

But the powerful Audit Committee, and later the board of Allied Irish Banks, which included some of the most eminent businessmen in Ireland and Britain, had decided to reject his thesis in favour of the 'Keogh Report' which exonerated the bank, accepted the doubtful amnesty and agreed that the scandal must be buried and the bank become 'forward looking' in its dealings with the Revenue and its tax-dodging customers.

Allied Irish Banks had its sights on one thing and one thing only – its ambitions. And the ambitions of its Chief Executive, were to make it the number one bank in the country. Its decision to turn a blind eye to the businessmen, farmers and commercial classes who had flocked to the bank to open bogus non-resident accounts had gone a long way to giving it the customer base to became just that. There was no room for a man as principled as Anthony Spollen in such a set-up. But where could he go?

When the board of AIB decided at their meeting on 27 May that what he had presented to the Audit Committee was an 'appalling vista' and they could not accept it, he was out of a job. In other circumstances he might have been quietly moved sideways, but he knew too much and the enmity between himself and the Chief Executive was, by now, far too deep. Spollen himself understood all this.

'I think, in fairness, Mr Culliton [Chairman of the Audit

Committee] didn't rubbish my figures. He said he really didn't consider my figures. Why? Because Mr Keogh is a very persuasive man and effectively he persuaded the Audit Committee of the bank that the bank had, in fact, an amnesty . . . Now that, to me, was an amazing job,' said Spollen long after these events had unfolded.

'But I think part of AIB's problem after ICI . . . there was a major problem in the bank in that when we had a difficulty with the regulators, any kind of difficulty, whether it was the share issue which was difficult . . . there was a problem in talking to the Central Bank and the Stock Exchange. In the UK, there was a reluctance to talk to the Bank of England. And this, to my view, was a pattern of behaviour, and I'm sad to say but I think one of the difficulties which came up in, I suppose, my discussions with Mr Scanlan . . . I think he had a tendency to see professional differences as personal differences. All this old baloney about me and my transfer and here I am compromising my professional integrity because I'm going to be transferred – this was the greatest red herring you could see.'

But the Chief Executive was looking at it from a completely different point of view. As Gerry Scanlan would later admit, it was a question of 'him or me'. Now Scanlan had come out on top, his writ would run right through the organisation, including the position of Group Internal Auditor.

Putting executive independence before the financial interests of the bank was Spollen's big mistake. When he was told what the board had decided, Spollen must have been bitterly disappointed. All through the crisis he had kept his counsel, talking only to Sutherland and Culliton, two men he trusted implicitly. But now it was over.

The Group Internal Auditor of AIB told his assistant, Don Walsh, that he would be leaving the bank. 'It was May 1991 when Mr Spollen told me himself for the first time that he was leaving the organisation. I had no indication up to that.' In some ways it was a relief because Walsh would say later that around that time, when the top secret letters and memos began to fly, he found Spollen difficult to deal with and a little more unpredictable than usual. This undoubtedly placed a strain on their relationship.

But Spollen had one advantage that most other executives who find themselves out on a limb might only dream about. His friend Peter Sutherland was intent on smoothing his exit. It was a difficult task, but for a man who had mastered the politics of the Law Library in Dublin, the corridors of power in Leinster House and the labyrinthine workings of the European Commission in Brussels, it was a worthy challenge. Sutherland also had the great advantage of knowing that, even though the past months had been bitter and stressful, Anthony Spollen was not a dissident or a sorehead. He would remain level-headed and a loyal company man to the end. He had too many friends in the social network of Dublin's business society to somehow turn rogue and become a true whistleblower.

Anthony Spollen had always placed discretion as one of his top priorities as a banker and as a person and that was why not even his oldest and closest friends would find out from him what had happened to precipitate his departure from one of the most important and sensitive jobs in Irish banking. As he said later, 'I kept my counsel.' And he meant it.

The need for secrecy was paramount. When relationships break down there is always the danger that one side or the other will be unreasonable. In such circumstances, that side often reaches for a lawyer and, almost without knowing it themselves, they are suddenly in the High Court in the full glare of publicity. After that, nothing in their lives is secret or sacrosanct again.

So, to prevent any leaks about the departure of Spollen, the negotiations to ease him out of the position of Group Internal Auditor and into early retirement were carried out largely in the large and comfortable drawing room of Peter Sutherland's gracious home on Eglington Road, Donnybrook, Dublin 4.

It was just a brisk walk from the Bankcentre in Ballsbridge where the drama had unfolded in the preceeding weeks and it was also discreet. Nobody would make much of the two men meeting there, after all it was well known among their circle that they were friends and often visited each other's homes for dinner parties and other pleasant social occasions.

Of course, Spollen wasn't the only casualty of the events that had unfolded in those early months of 1991. Coincidentally, John Keogh, his one-time friend who had failed to move Anthony Spollen as Group Internal Auditor on the instructions of Chief Executive Gerry Scanlan, also left the bank. Following Anthony Spollen's report to the Audit Committee, the relationship between the two men had become 'strained' according to Keogh, because he didn't agree with what Spollen had sent to the Audit Committee. It was also clear that Keogh, a director of AIB, had given the board a clear ultimatum: if they accepted his report then they had to get rid of Anthony Spollen. But, ironically, Keogh would leave a month before Spollen.

The best legal case, as Sutherland knew from experience, is one which never reaches the confines of a courtroom. Courts are unpredictable places and Sutherland required secrecy. That was why he so carefully conducted the negotiations that would sort out Spollen's departure in the comfortable surroundings of his own home.

After a series of meetings an 'exit package' was agreed. Spollen was to be paid a lump sum of over IR£500,000 and he was given an unspecified consultancy role with AIB for a number of years. There were also other possibilities of mutually beneficial business contacts promised for the coming years.

In return, he would leave the company and he would never speak of the events of early 1991 or the upheaval that these had caused in his life and in the life of Allied Irish Banks. The can was sealed with the smell safely inside. Or so they thought.

But as Peter Sutherland once wisely remarked in 1990, before any of these events began to trouble him: 'A significant number of people no longer want to sweep issues under the carpet – every time that happens now they rise from under the carpet.' It was a telling remark, in more ways than one.

Of course, from his work as a barrister and as a politician, Peter Sutherland was acutely aware that many things in Irish life, scandals and secrets, were locked away or shredded so that no-one would ever know the sordid details. It was a way of life and death for some. But he also foresaw that that era was coming to an end, although he had no indications then that he himself would become locked into one of the great secret scandals of the latter days of twentieth-century Ireland.

Peter Sutherland mixed with a lot of very important and influential people with different political and business agendas and, remarkably, they all liked him, valued his counsel and rewarded him. He was embedded in the 'Golden Circle' of the Ireland of the late 1980s and 1990s and yet he was above the corruption and scandals of that era. As he said himself, 'I've been lucky. I've been lucky all my life.' And luck was still with him as he negotiated the discreet exit of his friend Anthony Spollen in the middle of 1991 and ushered in a new order at Allied Irish Banks.

When he chaired the AGM of Allied Irish Banks on 11 July 1991 there was trouble enough, without the issue of bogus non-resident accounts surfacing to cause him trouble.

'We have seen a disquieting increase in the level of ill-informed comments about banks and banking, some of it directed at this bank,' he told shareholders with a straight face. 'The cheap jibe and the misleading headline about our business seems to command more attention than hard facts.'

The hard facts were that by that time a share in AIB was worth more than a share in Bank of Ireland – for the first time in the history of the Irish Stock Exchange. Rounding on the media and politicians during a 30-minute address to shareholders, he said that AIB was the 'oil that smoothly turns the wheels of industry, commerce, farming and life in general'.

There was something self-satisfied about his performance that day, but it was masterful given that by the time of the AGM he had just ushered the bank through one of the biggest crises in Irish banking history. Ironically, the following day, Cathal MacDomhnaill, Chairman of the Revenue Commissioners, presented the annual report of the Revenue to the then Minister for Finance, Albert Reynolds. There was an element of self-satisfaction about their performance too, although poorer tax returns for that year had resulted in higher government borrowings. After noting, among other things, that a Revenue investigation had yielded a tax payment of IR£530,000, he stated that, 'The improvement in compliance has been massive.'

Of course Reynolds was unaware of the IR£100 million tax liability at Allied Irish Banks which had been under the noses of the Revenue for several months and from which they would ultimately walk away from until their noses were rubbed in it seven years later.

Peter Sutherland knew the secret and knew too that the 'smell had been safely sealed in'. As he went on to greater things, the traumatic months of early 1991 may have even faded from his memory. But, as he said himself, 'Issues could no longer be swept under the carpet.'

Chapter 14

Murder in Malahide

With an amnesty in place after paying over IR£14 million to the Revenue Commissioners and the thorny question of Anthony Spollen out of the way following a large pay-off, Allied Irish Banks got back to what it did best: making money. Although they may have been slightly troubled about the events of the previous year, Peter Sutherland and Gerry Scanlan were not the kind of people to look back with regret or remorse.

The new buzzword on the fourth floor was 'going forward'. Those messy times of 1991 were now firmly in the past and the past was another country, and one best forgotten at that. The crisis had been averted and the once frightening possibility of damaging allegations being thrown around the Four Courts avoided. Of course these things had come with a price.

Spollen had been paid a golden handshake of nearly IR£500,000, a considerable sum at the time, to go away and guarantee his silence. But in the greater scheme of things it was a small price when considered against the IR£100 million AIB could have been required to pay.

Anthony Spollen could now settle down to write a book about 'corporate governance' in which he would write in general terms about international fraud, but make no reference to the huge problem that had been uncovered at his employer of 22 years. Nor would he ever reveal the details of what exactly happened in those tumultuous months, either before or after they become public knowledge. Spollen was, after all, a company man to the core.

The two men who had failed to move him on would also take leave of leafy Dublin 4. John Keogh, another of the main protagonists in the corporate war in AIB, left before Spollen, on terms which were never revealed. Brian Wilson would follow him in the years that followed.

The episode was over and the details safely sealed away in the bank vault.

But down in Nassau Street, in the headquarters of the Revenue Commissioners, not everybody was satisfied that all the information that had been accumulated about banks and bogus non-resident accounts had been used to their full potential. Tony McCarthy may have dumped his bank files on the floor and started trailing around the city after wealthy publicans but James Livingstone, head of the Special Inquiry Branch of the Revenue Commissioners, always believed that what had started in Milltown Malbay and Castlebar and the other tax-dodging towns of Ireland was 'unfinished business' for the banks and their customers. But Jimmy Livingstone was about to have troubles of his own.

On a cold blustery Monday, 7 December 1992, he walked out of his office in Nassau Street in central Dublin and went for a lunchtime stroll around the city. After finishing his day's work later that evening, he and a colleague drove home in the dark and the rain to The Moorings, the suburban estate near the entrance to the picturesque village of Malahide in north Dublin where he lived.

What greeted him when he arrived home at 5.50pm that evening was not a pretty sight, even for a hardened investigator and a seasoned hunter like Livingstone.

His 56-year-old wife Grace, bound and gagged with adhesive tape, was lying in a bloody mess on the bed in the upstairs bedroom of the house. She had been murdered. Her killer had taken one of Livingstone's guns from the cabinet and shot her at close range. On leaving, he had thrown the weapon into the shrubbery in the vicinity of the house where it was later found.

It was a shocking blow to Livingstone and his two children, Tara, who was 22 at the time and lived in Paris, and Conor, who was 20 and lived at home. But an even bigger shock to Livingstone was that he was suddenly the prime suspect in the investigation that followed.

That was the normal course of events in such cases. Most murders are committed by close relatives, but in Livingstone's case it was even more obvious why he was to come under the cold finger of suspicion. He was a gruff individual, not much given to taking anything lying down. He had a passionate interest in firearms and had an extensive collection of shotguns and pistols, some of them illegal. Without any other obvious suspect, he was targeted by the detectives investigating the case.

But he insisted, and his alibi seemed to bear him out, that he could account for every moment from the time he left his office in central Dublin to the time he arrived at his house that evening. He pointed out that he would not have had time to bind and gag his wife, callously shoot her, cover up the crime scene and go to a neighbour and raise the alarm in the short time between being dropped off by his work colleague and running to the neighbour's house to raise the alarm.

Jimmy Livingstone was also one of the most senior investigators in the Revenue Commissioners. He had an extensive knowledge of interrogation techniques and the methods used by investigating officers at a crime scene. He immediately began to insist to detectives that his wife was killed because of his work with revenue investigations which were then beginning to target money laundering by terrorists and other gangland figures. He even gave them names of underworld figures he had dealt with in his investigations, but this only served to make detectives more suspicious about him and his motives.

After being questioned on several occasions by detectives at Malahide Garda Station, investigators felt they were getting nowhere. Livingstone simply wouldn't answer their questions.

Then, on 2 March 1993, Livingstone was arrested at 7.30am and taken to Swords Garda Station where he was interrogated for two days. He said that within minutes of being processed and cautioned at the station, he was accused of murder. He later maintained that detectives taunted him for hours. They told him he was hated at work, especially by women colleagues, that neighbours were terrified of him because of his well-known obsession with weapons and firearms. He claimed that they also made derogatory remarks about the state of his marriage and his children.

Much later, when he eventually got access to more than 1,700 interviews conducted as part of the Garda investigation into the murder of his wife, he learned that his staff had said things that were generally favourable to him, and his neighbours, those that knew him, didn't speak ill of him.

With his activities in the FCA (the part-time wing of the Irish Army in which he was a high-ranking officer) and his boat on the Shannon, where he enjoyed fishing and shooting, he didn't spend much of his spare time in Malahide. Many of those living in The Moorings, a sprawling suburb built on a hill overlooking the estuary, didn't even realise that he was one of the most senior figures in the Revenue Commissioners.

Livingstone always maintained that he had a firm alibi that placed him either at work or on his way home with a work colleague when his wife was murdered. But he had great difficulty in convincing detectives of his whereabouts at the time of the crime.

As the investigation continued, it was revealed that Mrs Livingstone was last seen alive about 2pm that day by a neighbour. What intrigued detectives was that there was no sign of a break-in at the Livingstone's home. Nothing was taken. There appeared to be no motive for the killing of a simple housewife who went about her duties as a mother and homemaker and who wasn't known much outside her own family and social circle. It was a complete mystery why she, of all people, should have been murdered, and in such a cruel manner.

Although James Livingstone was the owner of three legally-held shotguns and a rifle, detectives discovered a cache of other handguns in the house. It later emerged that Livingstone, whose father was a jeweller, had a shed full of equipment for his hobby, which included modifying and making parts for guns. He was able to dismantle weapons in his collection, either modernising them or fitting new parts. It was precision work which would have been very difficult for the ordinary layman to carry out and his interest in such things was sure to raise suspicions.

'Although Mr Livingstone, the head of the Revenue Commissioners' Special Inquiry Branch, was investigating tax evasion linked to criminal activity, including money laundering, Gardaí believed it was likely that her killing was linked to his work,' said an early report by Paul O'Neill in *The Irish Times* the day after the murder.

He went on to say that because of the use of adhesive tape and the fact that Grace Livingstone was shot almost at point blank range by one of the two cartridges in the shotgun, the crime did have similarities with IRA 'execution' style murders.

Various newspaper reports linked James Livingstone with the work of the Special Inquiry Branch and revealed that in 1991 he had dealt with 1,323 detections for 'non-payment of tax' and that over 130 of these had been referred to the Revenue Commissioners' Special Investigation Branch whose remit had been widened that year to make it operationally more effective in dealing with tax evasion.

After he was arrested, the only thing that James Livingstone was charged with was possession of illegal firearms. In November 1993 he was fined IR£300 for illegally possessing an old Webley Mark VI revolver at his home. It was just one of a number of guns in his collection. It was later claimed that he had other weapons that the detectives never even knew about and that he destroyed some of these by sawing them up with a hacksaw, and handed over others as late as 2006 in an amnesty organised by Michael McDowell when he was Minister for Justice.

About a year after the arrest of Livingstone, the Garda Commissioner ordered a review of the original investigation of the murder of Grace Livingstone. A new team of detectives went in and began investigating the case from the beginning. Their findings were surprising.

The new investigation revealed a suspicious car in Malahide on the afternoon of the murder. But more significantly, it also revealed that the shotgun blast which killed Grace Livingstone was almost certainly fired in the late afternoon of that day.

The Gardaí identified four people who heard a loud bang, approximating a shot, in the area at about 4.30pm on the afternoon of her murder. They test-fired a weapon in the house and established that such a theory could be proven.

Most significantly of all, they discovered an unexplained thumb print on the adhesive tape used to bind the victim that did not match either Livingstone or his wife or any of the family. The murder of Grace Livingstone was never solved.

In the intervening years Livingstone and his two children

launched a long and torturous case against the Irish government and the Gardaí over their handling of the case. They accused the authorities of mismanaging the investigation and wrongly targeting him as a suspect.

On the mantelpiece of his living room a picture of his smiling wife Grace still has pride of place. His house contains box after box of files on the investigations, which he obtained through court orders to use in his own legal proceedings.

Surprisingly, perhaps, James Livingstone no longer believes that his work in the Special Inquiry Branch was a catalyst for the mysterious murder of his wife. But what happened that day in December 1992 certainly put an end to his career in the Irish Revenue Commissioners.

In the months that followed it became impossible for him to do his job and he was eventually transferred to international revenue investigations in Brussels where he worked until his retirement. He would later declare that the year it all happened was 'a very difficult year'. 'I had been falsely arrested by the guards on a capital charge of murder for killing my wife and I may not have been at my best at the time,' he said, explaining why his investigations after the tax evasion in Milltown Malbay and other towns had suddenly stalled.

Some people found the coincidence a bit too handy. The Revenue Commissioners had identified wholesale tax evasion in a couple of small Irish towns. They knew that evasion was rife, right across the country. Allied Irish Banks had suddenly settled for IR£14 million and the files had been thrown on the floor, the investigations had ceased and everybody had moved on.

But James Livingstone still believes that the banks had incited their customers to open bogus non-resident accounts around the country. He was just sorry that he had been transferred before he had time to open up the whole can of worms.

'Possibly my welfare was being considered and somebody thought maybe I should have a change,' he said in regard to his transfer. 'I don't know, I can make no deduction.'

It would be another five years before the whole question of bogus non-resident accounts would suddenly raise its ugly head again. In the meantime, the whole landscape of Ireland was being transformed. A controversial tax amnesty organised by Bertie Ahern led to the repatriation of billions of pounds back to Ireland. The tax rate fell from 65 per cent in 1985 to 56 per cent by 1990 and it kept falling until the memory of those penal days was almost forgotten.

Allied Irish Banks prospered, becoming one of the first billion pound companies in the State. Gerry Scanlan and the other directors became multi-millionaires on a mixture of executive pay and the lucrative share options they picked up as a reward for the huge profits the bank was making.

Peter Sutherland had resigned quite unexpectedly as Chairman of the bank and became the successful Chairman of the GATT (General Agreement on Trade and Tariffs) negotiations. After that triumph he went on to become International Chairman of the global merchant banking firm of Goldman Sachs.

All around Ireland the people who had once held bogus non-resident accounts were told by their banks to 'clean up their acts' and their accounts were largely reclassified. But as Allied Irish

Banks and the other banks and financial institutions reclassified most of these bogus accounts, much of the big money that was once hidden in them began to drain away into offshore accounts in secretive banking destinations like the Isle of Man and the Channel Islands.

Even the Revenue Commissioners were quietly satisfied. The problem of bogus non-resident accounts had been cleared without a whiff of scandal. The money was pouring in from the new buoyant Irish economy. So what could go wrong?

Everybody was 'forward looking' – well, everyone apart from one awkward customer. But what could one person do against the might of the establishment which had firmly put the lid on the can and sealed in the smell?

Chapter 15

Sunday Morning Coming Down

When Lochlann Quinn bought his newspapers on Sunday morning, 5 April 1998, he gazed at the front page of the *Sunday Independent* with what he later described as 'amazement'.

As one of Ireland's richest businessmen, the Chairman of Allied Irish Banks and one of the great art collectors of recent years, he was a man of the world. He might not have seen it all, but in his years as a financial accountant and major shareholder in the electrical multi-national Glen Dimplex, he had seen plenty.

Lochlann Quinn's first reaction that Sunday morning was to have a stiff drink, 'but the pubs weren't open'. Instead he walked back to his weekend retreat near Roundstone in Connemara. His weekend had just been ruined in a most unexpected way. Quinn, the owner of the prestigious Chateau de Fieuzal vineyard in southern France, may have had a glass of wine as he read the papers that Sunday morning, but it certainly didn't improve the taste in his mouth.

On the front page was a graphic with the AIB logo underneath a headline that shouted, 'AIB Had £600 Million In "Bogus" Accounts'. The story read:

> The largest bank in the country, Allied Irish Banks, had 53,000 bogus non-resident accounts containing nearly £600 million, a situation which a senior official described as 'frightening'.
>
> In a warning to the board of AIB in 1991, its internal auditor said 'the scale is staggering' and described the internal situation in the bank with bogus accounts as 'shocking'.
>
> The bogus accounts, which were spread through the bank's branch network, were used as a vehicle to avoid millions of pounds in tax.
>
> When the Group Internal Auditor, Mr Anthony Spollen, examined the situation in the bank, he identified 17,000 account holders who did not have proper authorisation to hold non-resident accounts and a further 36,000 account holders 'known to be bogus'.
>
> The Revenue Commissioners confirmed that they relied on the banks to make sure that such account holders were genuine. Explaining the situation, another senior bank executive described the problem of bogus accounts as 'an industry-wide problem'.
>
> In a report to the AIB Group Audit Committee in

March 1991, Anthony Spollen pointed out the gravity of the situation to the senior executives of AIB, including the Chairman of the group, Mr Peter Sutherland, and the Chief Executive, Mr Gerry Scanlan.

'The exposure of the group is, as stated above, substantial both in financial terms and in respect of the current tax codes,' he wrote.

The problem for AIB was so acute that it promised the Revenue Commissioners to make a 'determined effort' to clear up the problem by April 1990. But almost a year later the Revenue Commissioners gave the banks a further 'amnesty' until June 1991. At the time they warned: 'Detection of offences arising after that date will give rise to prosecution of both the bank and the officials involved.'

By the time he got down to this paragraph Lochlann Quinn knew that his bank was in serious trouble. The answers it had given to a series of questions from the *Sunday Independent* were feeble, at best.

Inside the newspaper was a 'backgrounder' on the whole affair and a trenchant commentary by columnist Gene Kerrigan who, as usual, got to the nub of the scandal with a few well chosen sentences:

Liam Collins' staggering story not alone discloses the extent of the criminality in which the AIB was involved – tens of thousands of bogus accounts – but reveals the maximum tolerance policies which the Revenue Commissioners and the Central Bank pursue towards certain types of crime.

The criminals and their accomplices who have been outed in recent times by the media, by *RTÉ News* and by the *Sunday Independent*, are not the snotty-nosed little addicts, permanent losers, at whom the politicians spew their venom. These are the people who attend each other's dinner parties; who give each other well-got information on horse racing and other forms of gambling; who propose one another for this club and that; their lawyers and accountants, their doctors and brokers, their agents and their art dealers. The people who take in each other's professional washing, cash in hand, nudge-nudge, wink-wink.

For Quinn the rest of the day was taken up with phone calls as he desperately tried to find out what had gone on in Allied Irish Banks back in 1991 and why hadn't he been told anything about it.

Or maybe he had. Even as he began to ask questions there was a niggling doubt in the back of his mind.

A small, gregarious man, fond of a glass of wine, he came from a family of upwardly mobile Dublin professionals and his more famous but less wealthy brother Ruairi was at this time leader of the Irish Labour Party. Ruairi had been Minister for

Finance up to the election the previous year and had since become leader of the party in succession to Dick Spring.

Lochlann Quinn lived between opulent homes in Dublin, the south of France and the west of Ireland. A Ferrari-driving accountant, he and partner Martin Naughton had made their millions with the Glen Dimplex brand. Both men also became huge investors in Irish art, along with other prominent businessmen like Tony O'Reilly, Michael Smurfit and Tony Ryan as they sent the prices of Yeats, Lavery and other well-known painters through the roof while vying to increase their collections.

Quinn and Naughton also developed the five-star Merrion Hotel in which many of their paintings hang. This allowed Quinn to avail of a tax break which was put in the Finance Act while brother Ruairi was Minister for Finance.

'I did call Tom Mulcahy [AIB Chief Executive] on Monday morning and said, you know, "Can we have a chat?"' Lochlann Quinn later recalled.

Mulcahy himself admitted that he was just as shocked at what he had read in Sunday morning's papers as anyone else. 'A lot of us were discovering about an issue that we weren't familiar with for the first time in the context of what was in the *Sunday Independent*.'

Quinn too maintained, 'The first I ever heard of the DIRT issue was in the *Sunday Independent* article.'

But that wasn't quite true.

As the bank's massive public relations machine went into overdrive to try and salvage something from the disaster that had befallen them that Sunday morning, Lochlann Quinn was quietly reminded of a little chat he had had with the outgoing Chairman of AIB when he took over the job from Jim Culliton in 1997. (Culliton had stepped in when Peter Sutherland left suddenly in 1993 to chair the riveting Uruguay round of talks on the General Agreement on Trade & Tarriffs (GATT).) He recalled:

> I think in the briefing I got there was about five minutes on the fact that there had been an issue over Mr Spollen's departure from the bank, but it lasted about five minutes. I think the briefing I got from Jim Culliton spanned, I suppose, about an hour and a half and covered all sorts of things, half them being, I guess, the future of the bank rather than the past. But he referred to a couple of things because I, being newly on the board, really knew nothing about most of the history of the bank.

Quinn also maintained, probably correctly, that although he was in business in Dublin he had never heard much about the subject of bogus non-resident accounts, which were more of a phenomenon outside the capital among the professional classes, farmers and shopkeepers in the big towns and the hidden Ireland, fast disappearing. He maintained:

> Looked at from the bank's point of view the issue was over, the issue had ended in 1991. It was history, so the fact that it resurfaced was clearly a

difficulty.

You know, you come in as Chairman in 1997. How far back do you go with issues that are over? I mean the real issue is: what's the future, not the past?

It was also a shock for Mulcahy, who coincidentally had presided over the infamous 'Dana Affair' but seemed unaware of the consequences in the upper echelons of the bank and the rift it had caused between Anthony Spollen and Gerry Scanlan. But now that he was in charge, Mulcahy had to deal with the fallout from a much bigger disaster.

'The first thing I'd to do was to go and try to find a copy of the documents which I was reading about in the newspapers. That's as much as I knew about it. Because when I took over from Mr Scanlan he would have briefed me in the same way as our Chairman was briefed by Mr Culliton and it didn't register on any scale,' claimed Mulcahy.

Although both Scanlan and Culliton had been at the centre of the shocking events of 1991, both believed that it was all over and it would never resurface. They believed that Sutherland and Spollen had reached an agreement that would guarantee secrecy on the upheavals which had taken place in 1991. The bank's settlement with Spollen, not to mention his own natural discretion, would ensure that.

Even worse, the revelations in the *Sunday Independent* had come just three weeks before the Annual General Meeting of the bank. The annual report had already gone for printing and there was no mention of DIRT or bogus non-resident accounts in it. Nor would there be.

The AGM was already promising to be stormy enough with expected input from dissident shareholders and former employees like Niall Murphy who enjoyed causing havoc when the occasion arose. Because they had been haranguing directors for years Murphy and his ilk were portrayed as 'cranks' in the media. But the story in the *Sunday Independent* proved that they weren't the crackpots that the bank had made them out to be and also provided perfect ammunition to be used at the AGM as a stick with which to beat the bank.

As Murphy said of that Sunday when he opened his newspaper: 'It was one of the happiest days of my life.'

But for Lochlann Quinn it was another story. He explained:

Because I had to get into the detail of this to go before the AGM and say to the shareholders I didn't – you know – that this was not a problem, so I had to, in effect, carry out, at that particular stage, my own investigation within the bank.

From the contemporaneous evidence of the conversations that all our people had with the Revenue, it was quite clear that we in the bank did not know – this is correct – what the scale of the problem was. We knew there was a problem but we didn't know the scale of it, it had never been measured. And it followed on when I looked at those files, and looked at the behaviour of the

Revenue, we had told the Revenue that, subsequent to a re-categorisation, substantial increases in our DIRT payments would result. There were substantial increases in our DIRT payments and the Revenue never came back to us.

It was clear to me, at that particular stage, taking the detailed contemporaneous notes of our own staff, followed by the Revenue's behaviour . . . I mean, they walked away. I mean it wasn't a case that they walked away not knowing the figures were there.

So we never got an assessment, never got a demand, never got a telephone call. So, I was reasonably confident that the Revenue was reasonably informed that there had been a historic problem.

The correction of our DIRT payments made it very clear to the Revenue that we had got our act together. And they never sent in an assessment, never lifted the phone – did nothing.

So it wasn't only the bankers who were having an uncomfortable Sunday morning. The incoming Chairman of the Revenue Commissioners, Dermot Quigley, was also struggling to find out what exactly went on between his office and AIB in 1991. The more he heard, the more unpleasant he began to feel.

The 'little people', the ordinary taxpayers, were finding out that a huge tax scandal in Ireland's biggest bank had been within the grasp of the Revenue Commissioners back in 1991, but instead of closing in for the kill they had walked away, letting the bank off absolutely free. Revenue then took their best investigators off the case and put them to the tough job of going around the bars, squeezing a few high profile bar owners who were driving flashy cars and living ostentatious lifestyles.

The Revenue Commissioners liked taxes that were easy to collect – PAYE which was deducted by employers and DIRT which was turned in by the banks. After that they didn't make waves.

As former Minister for Finance Albert Reynolds said, 'A messenger on a bicycle could collect more tax on Ailesbury Road than the Revenue Commissioners managed to collect on the property tax.'

Ruairi Quinn commented: 'I do not recall any occasion on which the question of evasion of DIRT or the widespread existence of bogus non-resident accounts was raised.'

You would think that if there was such a large pot of gold out there, someone would have told the Minister for Finance. But the issue was never raised and Revenue never bothered to collect IR£100 million in unpaid taxes at AIB.

If ever there was an 'appalling vista' here it was, splashed across the front page of Ireland's biggest selling newspaper.

Chapter 16

A Second Amnesty, Perhaps

As he sat behind his desk in Dublin Castle on 6 April 1998, the Chairman of the Revenue Commissioners, Cathal Mac Domhnaill, had a lot to think about. But principally he was cogitating how he would proceed after reading the story about Allied Irish Banks in the previous day's *Sunday Independent*.

The shocking story that internal documents from Allied Irish Banks showed that it had 53,000 bogus accounts containing IR£600 million in 1991 was an unwelcome intrusion into the well ordered world of collecting taxes. Mac Domhnaill was just a couple of months away from retirement and a crisis of this magnitude was not something he welcomed in the twilight of his career. It was also a surprise to many of those who had spent their lives in the Revenue Commissioners.

'If the dogs in the street know about it, how come I didn't?' asked Phillip Curran, a former Revenue Chairman.

'I think to move from the general to the more specific, in terms of the specific disclosures in relation to AIB and, of course, other financial institutions, which were dealt with in the [*Sunday*] *Independent* article, certainly Revenue did not have that information until it became public,' said Dermot Quigley, who was shortly to assume the mantle of Chairman.

After a number of fairly leisurely internal meetings and phone calls, the strategy was agreed among senior officials. Never ones to get unduly worked up about what they read in the newspapers, the Investigation Branch of Revenue finally got around to writing to the Chief Executive of Allied Irish Banks, Gerry Scanlan, on 16 April, ten days after precise details of unprecedented allegations of tax evasion by the bank and its customers had been published.

This letter to Scanlan, mild in tone, referred to 'the media reports' and asked for a report on non-compliance with DIRT by the bank. As a result of this letter a series of meetings was arranged. Tom Tiuit, Principal Inspector of Taxes, and Paddy Donnelly from his department in the Revenue Commissioners sat across the table from the bank's two tax experts, Philip Brennan, Head of Group Taxation, and Deirdre Fullen, Tax Compliance Manager.

As is customary with these things, each side had different objectives. The Revenue Commissioners wanted to see *Octopus,* Spollen's original report from 1991 which contained a series of damning allegations against the bank. Although extracts of this and other internal bank documents had appeared for two successive Sundays in the *Sunday Independent*, they had been edited for legal reasons. Revenue were now looking to examine the original document.

The executives from Allied Irish Banks had a completely different objective – they wanted to get the £100 million tax liability mentioned in Spollen's documentation 'off the table'.

According to Philip Brennan, the *Spollen Report*, as it became known, was handed over to Revenue Commissioners at the second of this series of meetings. On 8 May 1998 the Investigation Branch wrote to the bank based on its initial examination of the documents saying that they would have expected that all relevant facts would have been disclosed to Revenue 'at the appropriate time' [1991] and pointing out they were now owed a huge amount of money. Or, as they put it more delicately in civil service language, 'non-compliance issues now require to be addressed'.

On 21 May 1998, AIB replied, expressing 'fundamental' disagreement with the Revenue's belief that the bank now had a debt of IR£100 million as calculated by Mr Spollen back in 1991.

On 4 June, the Investigation Branch wrote back 'refuting the bank's contentions':

> Your fundamental contentions are not accepted. I have checked with the officers involved and I am not in doubt about the matter. There was substantial material non disclosure. A further letter will be sent to you in due course.
> Yours faithfully
> T M Tiuit, Principal Inspector of Taxes

But there the matter seemed to rest. Astonishingly, there was no further correspondence for several months.

The public, the media and the politicians might have expected the Revenue Commissioners to seize the initiative and put Allied Irish Banks under enormous pressure – especially since they had been handed all the evidence they required on a plate. But no, if anything the Revenue Commisioners seemed embarrassed by the newspaper disclosures which left them looking inefficient and flat footed. It seemed to many observers that Revenue simply wanted the whole scandal to disappear quietly.

That is exactly what seemed to be happening. There was a distinct sigh of relief in AIB's Bankcentre in leafy Dublin 4. But Tom Tiuit hadn't quite gone away, as the bankers hoped. He was trying to find exactly who knew what back in the early months of 1991 when secret negotiations were taking place within the bank and with the Revenue Commissioners. It wasn't easy.

So Tiuit began to court the 'source' – the bank's troublesome Internal Auditor, Anthony Spollen.

The dilemma that the Irish tax authorities found themselves with was that AIB had a 15-page contemporaneous note of what went on, while the Revenue Commissioners had very little apart from their memories. Crucially, Allied Irish Banks had a contemporaneous note of a phone conversation between its top tax man, Jimmy O'Mahony, and the Revenue investigator, Tony McCarthy. McCarthy had no recollection of this conversation, 'if it every took place at all'.

Almost like a figure from a Le Carré novel, Tiuit was trying to become Anthony Spollen's 'handler' so that he could get the inside story. But Spollen, who was now an AIB pensioner, was a reluctant whistleblower.

'He called me many times,' remembered Spollen. 'I said I couldn't . . . he wanted, I think, to bring a colleague to meet me. I said no, I could not do that. I said I would only do it if he were to call the bank and say, you know, would you . . . I'd like to meet Tony Spollen together with . . . He called me a fair few times because he was anxious. And I think the question which he posed to me was, in my opinion – I think this was the question – did I believe that we would, the bank, would have known the scale of the problem, would know there was a large problem at 13 February [1991] and I concluded, yes that we would have known it was a large problem.'

But Spollen steadfastly refused to talk. The only person he confided in was his wife. So when Tiuit went on holidays for the month of August the whole affair seemed to have died down.

Philip Brennan, head of Taxation in AIB, now began to believe that because of the 'non-follow up' of correspondence by Revenue the matter had been dropped. 'You will note that the letter promises that they would – the Revenue would – be in contact with us further. The Revenue didn't get in contact with us further until October,' he would explain later.

July, August and September 1998 passed and there was a sense of relief among the top men in Allied Irish Banks. But Brennan had other reasons to believe the almost unbelievable, that Revenue were going to walk away from the whole affair.

To an outsider it might seem blindingly obvious that if Allied Irish Banks owed a pot of gold in back taxes, Revenue and their political masters would be only too anxious to collect it. But that does not take into account the civil service mentality. The question that now arose was how could this ever have been allowed to happen in the first place and, more importantly, who was going to take the blame? The one way of avoiding these awkward questions was to do nothing, which is what seemed to be happening.

But there was yet another reason for AIB believing it was going to walk away free from the greatest financial scandal in the history of the State. There were also informal 'communications' going on behind the scenes. Some people believed that they could achieve 'an Irish solution to an Irish problem' as it were.

Dr Donal de Buitléir, who had worked in the Revenue Commissioners but had been headhunted like many of his colleagues by Allied Irish Banks, was now Group Manager in the office of the Chief Executive Officer of AIB. For 20 years he and an old friend, Sean Moriarty, Assistant Secretary in the Revenue Commissioners, had been dining together informally every couple of months. Moriarty was the author of the infamous report which had been shelved by his bosses in Revenue.

When de Buitléir left Revenue, Moriarty got his job. They kept in contact and served on a government committee and were 'involved in another organisation' together so they had remained good friends.

Moriarty was just the kind of friend you could pick up the telephone and call for an informal chat when things were 'hotting up' on a particular issue.

'I had discussions with Mr Moriarty of the Revenue

Commissioners – I just can't recall when, June or July, when we discussed this matter and perhaps other matters, it was very current at the time. And his view – and I can't recall exactly what he might have said – was that this matter would probably be okay. He didn't – I don't think he was definitive about it,' said Dr de Buitléir later.

Neither of the two men had 'functional responsibility' for the issue at the time, but at their meetings in the restaurant in the National Gallery or the nearby University Club (they could not be certain about the venue) they certainly discussed the great events of the day and this one in particular.

Like all good executives, de Buitléir reported back to Philip Brennan, Head of Group Taxation, the detail of his contacts. Brennan regarded his reports as very favourable – Revenue and the bank were going to bury the issue, he believed. Neither side really wanted the dirt to come out publicly, they both stood to lose a lot.

'I formed the view from – I can't exactly remember the words he used to me – but I formed the view from what he [de Butléir] told me, together with the fact that there had been no – the Revenue hadn't reverted to us, that the matter had been satisfactorily resolved,' said Brennan.

Moriarty was less than happy with this recollection of events by his friend. If he realised the lunch conversations he was having were being related back to the bank's top executives, which is doubtful, he certainly didn't concur with the conclusions.

'When the investigation began, certainly the people on the

investigation side asked me for my memory of the thing at the time and I told them what I remembered about it at the time. I certainly wasn't in a position, nor did I offer any comfort to Dr de Buitléir or AIB. I just wasn't in a position to,' he said later, when the matter came to be publicly investigated.

But oddly enough Philip Brennan was not the only one who thought AIB were off the hook. His contention seemed to be borne out by others. After the story broke, Margaret Walsh, a partner in the influential Dublin accountancy firm Price Waterhouse Cooper and external auditor of AIB, was closely involved in advising the bank about their problem and what, if any, documentation should be handed over to the Revenue Commissioners. During meetings with AIB personnel she compiled a series of notes which would lead to a great deal of controversy. Among them was the following:

'After publication of the original story in the *Sunday Independent* they [AIB] had discussions with the Revenue and thought the matter had been satisfactorily resolved,' she noted.

This contention was also supported by Noel Glennon, Chief Corporate Tax Manager of AIB. 'It would have been our impression that the passage of time had elapsed where there was no further contact in relation to the previous meetings that had taken place – that we had formed the impression that matters had been resolved, that there was no follow-up,' he said.

In other words, AIB now believed that they had achieved a second amnesty. They had paid off Revenue with IR£14 million in 1991 to get out of a debt that they believed themselves was IR£100 million. Now, in 1998, they believed they were pulling off a second stunt, this time walking away without paying a cent because the original deal still stood. This 'absolution' was granted to them, they believed, because they had 'extensive file notes' of the meetings in 1991, but all Revenue had to rely on was the memory of Tony McCarthy, the man who had been taken off the investigation just when it seemed the bank was about to crack.

'Our belief then was that we had an arrangement. Our belief now is we have an arrangement. And added to that the absence of contact for a period, we viewed or had the impression that we haven't heard in months so obviously there may be an acceptance of the deal,' maintained Noel Glennon.

But Margaret Walsh of PWC went further. Although she did not attend the meetings she was briefed afterwards, and her notes indicated that everything was going well until there was a sudden phone call from the new Chairman of the Revenue Commissioners. Her file note read: 'The correspondence ceased with an expression that Revenue would be in contact with us further, but no further contact happened. However, they [AIB] had received a sudden phone call from Dermot Quigley, the new Chairman of the Revenue Commissioners.'

As it happens, Dermot Quigley had succeeded Cathal Mac Domhnaill as Chairman of the Revenue Commissioners in July but it was October before he got around to the 'sudden phone call'.

Walsh later retracted this note, as did Philip Brennan.

But there were other problems on the horizon. The Oireachtas Committee of Public Accounts was due to meet on 15 September and on its agenda was the issue of banks and bogus non-resident accounts. Added to that, a reporter from *Magill* magazine, Ursula Halligan, was putting questions to both AIB and the Revenue Commissioners based on the same set of documents that had been the basis for the series of *Sunday Independent* exclusives the previous April.

The day the story appeared in *Magill*, Donal de Buitléir from the Chief Executive's Office in AIB was 'in contact' with the Revenue press office at a high level. AIB's taxation boss, Philip Brennan, was talking to Tom Tiuit in Revenue as he tried to guess where the story was going. Almost immediately there was another media firestorm. It was as if the story was brand new.

Suddenly the Revenue investigation which had been stalled for months was very much 'on' again as they came under ferocious pressure from the public and their political masters, who were now seriously unhappy that six months after the story had broken nothing appeared to have happened.

Magill had also published huge chunks of the documents which the *Sunday Independent* had been advised by lawyers not to use because these were internal letters and memoranda. But these gave the story a whole new lease of life and added spice to the drama.

When the story surfaced for the second time in October 1998, I came under pressure, as the person who had broken the original story, to come up with another 'exclusive'. So the following week's *Sunday Independent* caused another furore.

Under the headline 'Meeting To Axe AIB Whistleblower In Sutherland's Home', it read:

> The accountant who blew the whistle within Allied Irish Banks on the £600 million worth of bogus non-resident accounts in the bank was effectively removed from his position as Group Internal Auditor after a series of secret meetings, some of which were held in the home of the bank's then Chairman, Mr Peter Sutherland.
>
> The *Sunday Independent* has learned that following serious internal differences among senior executives of the bank, two directors, Chairman Peter Sutherland and Jim Culliton, a former chief executive of CRH, were brought in to negotiate a severance deal for AIB's Group Internal Auditor, Anthony Spollen.

When the story appeared Peter Sutherland was furious. That Sunday evening I got a call at home from a very worried Chief Executive of Independent Newspapers, David Palmer. Palmer had been running the Independent Group for about two years, and during that time I may have had one or two short conversations with him, but he certainly was not in the habit of phoning me at home. Now, he was calm but definite.

'That story is very dangerous,' he told me that Sunday night in October. 'I am told that Peter Sutherland is with his lawyers at the moment deciding what course of action to take.'

I was worried.

He asked me if I could stand over the story and emphasised that in terms of big business, it would not be considered appropriate to conduct such negotiations in one's home. I told him that business in Ireland was not always conducted in the same formal way as it might be in the City of London and said I was pretty certain of the story before putting the phone down.

But I was very worried, both at getting a phone call like that at home and also because Peter Sutherland was a very important person in the world by 1998. He had gone on to become Chairman of merchant bank Goldman Sachs International and a director of the giant oil company, BP.

He was not a man I wished to tangle with.

In something of a panic I rang my contact and explained the phone call I had received and the news that Sutherland was consulting with his lawyers on a Sunday night. There was a brief silence.

'Sutherland fucks with you, we'll fuck with Sutherland,' he said and that was the end of the conversation.

The following week a number of stories appeared in the newspapers after 'briefings' by a close associate of Peter Sutherland, a very distinguished public relations executive who acts for some of the most important people in Ireland and is drafted in by AIB in times of crisis.

This faceless person denied to reporters that any such meetings took place in Sutherland's home and the stories were duly printed in the daily papers. I smiled ruefully.

A couple of weeks later I met my contact in Gibney's bar in Malahide, a nice village in north Dublin where many of the locals appear to be multi-millionaires and like to flaunt their wealth with huge mansions that are visible from the road and glittering lifestyles to go with them.

I began to whinge about the stories that had appeared.

'Don't worry about it. Who cares?' he said. 'But I can tell you that the story is true. The deal was done in Sutherland's house. And why not? Weren't they friends? That's the way they were able to keep the lid on the whole thing.'

There was no statement from Anthony Spollen in response to this story.

Now Dermot Quigley began to personally take charge of the investigation. Allied Irish Banks got an ultimatum to have information available for Revenue within two weeks. Things were beginning to move. The Oireachtas Committee of Public Accounts, chaired by Jim Mitchell TD, decided to call Dermot Quigley before its session on 13 October 1998.

The afternoon before he was due to go in to be questioned by TDs and Senators who were members of the Oireachtas Committee of Public Accounts in Leinster House, Dr Donal de Buitléir of Allied Irish Banks called to see Quigley in Dublin Castle. The meeting was brief and to the point.

De Buitléir made the Chairman of the Revenue Commissioners aware that AIB had a 15-page note of its meeting on 13 February 1991 between the two sides. This, he informed the Revenue boss, would be the basis for the bank's claim that it had settled with Revenue for IR£14 million and both sides had agreed that 'going forward' it had an amnesty.

It was a vital piece of information and Dr de Buitléir said he would have to make it known to the Committee that was investigating the whole bogus account story.

But the story was about to take another twist.

Chapter 17

Committee Room Deliberations

Although his son worked for Allied Irish Banks in London, Fine Gael politician Jim Mitchell was determined that his investigations into the Irish banking system and the use of bogus non-resident accounts was going to be a landmark in Irish parliamentary democracy.

After the initial furore in April, when the story was first published in the *Sunday Independent,* until the autumn of 1998, it seemed that nothing further was going to happen. Revenue was bogged down trying to extract information from AIB and its former Internal Auditor, Anthony Spollen. Senior figures within the bank and its auditors, the influential firm of PWC, were convinced that the whole scandal was simply going to disappear again like a puff of smoke. Indeed some senior political figures were also coming to the conclusion that some sort of an arrangement had been arrived at to allow AIB and other financial institutions off the hook.

But two things happened that autumn to upset any cosy arrangement that might have been developing.

In October, on the eve of a meeting of the Public Accounts Committee of the Dáil at which senior bankers in Allied Irish Banks were to be questioned, *Magill* magazine, run by the campaigning Vincent Browne, revived the story.

Always in pursuit of a good story, his magazine had acquired the same set of internal AIB documents as had initially made their way into my hands. The magazine's dogged reporter Ursula Halligan re-wrote the DIRT story, dramatising the events with pictures and the names of the main players. She had also put a series of awkward questions to Peter Sutherland and other board members of Allied Irish Banks in 1991, to Dermot Quigley, Chairman of the Revenue Commissioners and to leading figures in the Central Bank. The response, or lack of it, was illuminating.

Her report also raised for the first time Anthony Spollen's calculation that AIB could have a tax liability of IR£100 million, which was a new and dramatic twist to the story. It made for devastating headlines and the series of denials and 'no comments' from the bankers and the Revenue officials involved left 'official Ireland' looking foolish, incompetent and clearly turning a blind eye to a huge tax fraud.

Faced with further lurid headlines and a public outcry from politicians as the story took legs for a second time, various powerful interests in the government, the Revenue Commissioners and the banks began to take up positions to try to distance themselves from the scandal and subsequent cover-up of 1991.

This was compounded on 13 October 1998 when Dermot Quigley went before the Public Accounts Committee of the Dáil and stated that he was 'unaware of the scale of bogus non-resident accounts in AIB until the media disclosures in April 1998'. He also insisted that there had been no deal between the bank and the Revenue in respect of unpaid DIRT.

Two days later the Chief Executive of AIB, Tom Mulcahy, was in fighting form when he told the Committee that the issue of bogus accounts was 'an industry wide problem rather than a problem that was specific to Allied Irish Banks'. He insisted that the banks were all in this together, hoping, probably, that faced with such a major challenge the authorities would do what they usually did and back away from a full-scale confrontation.

Mulcahy, who in his previous existence had presided over the 'Dana' fiasco at AIB, then sought to transfer the blame from the bank to its customers, stating:

> Across Ireland, and indeed across other countries, many savers sought confidentiality and had an aversion to paying tax on interest. It should be noted that it was the saver who had the aversion to paying tax on interest. There was a long standing background of residents masquerading as non-residents in order to do this. There was sensitivity in successive governments to tackling the problem due to the legitimate fear of a flight of funds and the resulting effects on a fragile economy.

But he also insisted that senior executives of the bank and the Revenue Commissioners had reached a deal, an unofficial amnesty back in 1991 to solve the problem. The bank did have one stumbling block, however. It had notes of meetings with senior Revenue people, notably Tony McCarthy, but no documents which spelled out definitively that they had agreed an amnesty.

'Another interpretation of this situation is that it suited nobody to put it in writing,' said Jim Mitchell, Chairman of the Public Accounts Committee.

'It is an extraordinary thing for banks, who get everything in writing, and have it all spelt out if they are lending money to anybody, that the AIB did not get this in writing. There was a wink and a nod here and that is what is being put forward,' he said.

It was, according to a tetchy Tom Mulcahy, 'a traditional agreement', whatever that was.

But the bank never tried to find out whether Spollen's IR£100 million figure was, as they liked to describe it, 'off the wall' or not. They did some calculations of their own and came up with a figure of IR£35 million, but because they now believed they had an amnesty they simply filed this away, hoping never to have to pull it out of the cabinet again. Once they got rid of Spollen they thought they had also got shut of the problem and went back to doing what they did best, making astronomical profits and paying their top executives huge salaries and bonuses.

'Due to the forward looking nature of the arrangement entered into in good faith with Revenue, we did not quantify the extent of the problem [in 1991], nor were we asked to quantify it. The emphasis was on getting things right for the future,' insisted Mulcahy. He went one step further in attacking his former colleague Anthony Spollen, saying his figures 'included in the leaked documentation' were 'overestimations and seriously unreliable'.

Mulcahy went on to allege that Anthony Spollen's interest in the issue 'became very active' once he learned that AIB's Jimmy O'Mahony was 'in dialogue' with Revenue. The figure of IR£100 million owed to the government was 'without foundation' according to Philip Brennan of the Taxation Department of AIB.

After the bad-tempered meeting of the Public Accounts Committee, the government of the day, led by Taoiseach Bertie Ahern, who as Minister for Finance in 1993 had approved a controversial tax amnesty himself, was now forced to take action.

On 21 October 1998, the Dáil passed a resolution requesting the Public Accounts Committee to investigate the issue of bogus non-resident accounts. On 8 December, a Bill, which became legislation ten days later, was introduced in the Dáil allowing for the investigations to take place and giving immunity to witnesses who appeared before it. More importantly, it authorised the Comptroller and Auditor General (CAG), John Purcell, to lead the preliminary investigations. He was, it said: 'To ascertain if there was a shortfall in the amounts of DIRT paid by the financial institutions and the reasons for and the circumstances of the shortfall.' The scope of the investigations was confined to the years from 1 January 1986 to 1 December 1998.

Once the enabling legislation was passed, a dedicated team

comprising staff from within the Comptroller's office with expertise in accounting, information technology and legal affairs was set up to undertake the investigation work. It was a huge task, but with virtually unlimited legal powers it began to interview senior figures from the banks, the Revenue and the authorities under oath. It also began to trawl through banking records using legal powers to obtain confidential and secret files, and other material from the various financial institutions.

The report, which emerged in July 1999, was devastating in its scope, revealing the culture of greed and tax evasion at the heart of Irish society. It also illustrated how the banks and other financial institutions colluded and competed for 'hot money' in virtually every town and village in Ireland where there was more than one bank.

For the first time an official government report also revealed how the regulators, the tax authorities and the Department of Finance had 'sat idly by' while all this was going on in a country where hospital wards were being closed because there wasn't enough money to run them properly.

The 371-page report which was followed by hundreds of pages of appendices came to no conclusions but, taken with the earlier reports in the *Sunday Independent* and later in *Magill*, the picture it set out was one which could not be ignored.

While all this was going on, Jim Mitchell had been working away in the background to construct a public inquiry that would follow the publication of the report. The highly ambitious Mitchell had been frozen out of the Fine Gael front bench by its new party leader John Bruton. With the committee, he found an outlet for his talents and would go on to preside over a model investigation that will probably never be repeated.

When the committee began its deliberations in September 1999, he added the unusual coup of having the public sessions of the committee televised by the Irish language television service TG4 so that people could sit in the comfort of their own homes and watch a parade of influential civil servants, senior businessmen and politicians as they were interrogated about their activities. For some people it seemed the first indication of successful democracy at work and, for a short time at least, it countered growing public cynicism towards politicians and their activities.

Mitchell was a former Minister for Justice and an influential and popular politician across the political spectrum. Probably his two closest and most able lieutenants in what became a ground-breaking investigation were Labour Party TD Pat Rabbitte and the colourful Fianna Fáil TD, Sean Doherty, who had been sacked as Minister for Justice from Charlie Haughey's government for authorising illegal wire taps of journalists' phones.

But Doherty had another skill that was to prove invaluable – he had been a detective in Roscommon before going into politics. He knew 'how things worked' and how to 'draw out' a suspect in interrogation. His focus was not on the businessmen and farmers who dodged tax, but on the culture at the very top of the banks which allowed it to happen.

Mitchell, Rabbitte and Doherty all emerged from the inquiry with enhanced reputations because of their grasp of the subject, their probing questions and their refusal to accept 'no' for an answer from some of the most powerful people in the country.

But the political investigations also mirrored much of Irish life. Another member of the committee was the Fianna Fáil TD for Kerry, Denis Foley. Later in 2000, before the committee submitted its final report, it was revealed that Foley was a tax-dodging holder of an offshore Ansbacher account himself.

Foley had all the appearances of a country TD rather than a suave and shrewd Kerry businessman. But he admitted that Charlie Haughey's accountant Des Traynor had told him in the mid-1970s that he would get him a good return if he could raise £50,000. Foley, who had acted during his political career as Chairman of the Public Accounts Committee before Jim Mitchell, raised the money 'from his own resources' and at one stage his investment was worth £82,000.

He said that before 1995 the only documentation he had received from Traynor did not indicate where the money was held, except that it was with Klic Investments Ltd. Foley said later his financial affairs were handled by Pádraig Collery and later John Furze. At one stage when he queried Traynor because there was no letterheading on a statement of account, he was told it was 'for security reasons'.

'Deputy Foley accepted that, while he, at the time, did not know for certain that his money was in an Ansbacher account, a reasonable person knowing those facts – the involvement of Mr Traynor and Mr Collery, the mention of Mr Furze's name, the emergence of the information at the McCracken Tribunal – ought to have concluded, as a matter of probability, that his money was so invested,' he said in a statement, drafted by his legal advisors.

Another member of the committee who was to become more celebrated in the years that followed was Beverley Cooper-Flynn TD, the daughter of the powerful Fianna Fáil figure, Pádraig Flynn from Castlebar, Co Mayo. Eventually she had to resign from the committee after it was revealed that in her previous life as an employee of National Irish Banks, where she had worked prior to being elected to the Dáil in 1998, she had sold 'single premium insurance policies' to wealthy clients of the bank to allow them to take money 'offshore' and evade tax.

When the NIB scandal was broken by RTÉ reporters Charlie Bird and George Lee in January 1998, there was just a passing reference to Cooper-Flynn. But in the months that followed, Charlie Bird discovered that her involvement was greater than he had thought.

A wealthy farmer claimed that the newly elected TD had advised him not to avail of the 1993 tax amnesty but to invest his money through her with National Irish Bank. 'James Howard said he had met Cooper-Flynn at the NIB branch in Balbriggan in May 1993. He had undeclared income. She pushed him to invest in the CMI [Clerical Medical Insurance] scheme,' he said in his book, *This is Charlie Bird*.

The resulting report of June 1998 led to a celebrated High Court libel action against Charlie Bird and RTÉ which Beverley Cooper-Flynn lost. The jury decided that it was not proved that she sold the offshore policy to Howard, but found she had encouraged other people to evade their taxes as a result of her work with NIB. She subsequently appealed to the Supreme Court and lost again – running up a bill for nearly €2.5 million, which she settled in 2007 for €1.5 million, leading to a major public outcry.

Cooper-Flynn's defence, that she was only doing her job, deserves some sympathy. It seems ironic that a small cog in a small bank should have had to bear most of the public ire for the scandal when fat cat directors of all the major banks and financial institutions, many of whom became millionaires, got away without a stain on their characters. In some notable cases, they were even appointed to State boards and prominent positions in the financial world for their troubles.

But such matters were unknown when the Dáil committee set out to unravel the events that began back in the 1980s and culminated in 1998 with media reports of the scale of tax evasion by AIB and its customers. It was a complex task.

The picture that emerged was that bogus non-resident accounts were used throughout the country by people who wanted to evade tax. The banks were only too willing to help them because they got access to customers with money and could pay them less interest than normal depositors. The banks and building societies were also competing with each other for customers and if one bank wasn't willing to help a customer evade tax that customer simply went up the street where another bank was only too ready to facilitate them.

The Central Bank, instead of regulating the banks, acted as a kind of head office for them, more concerned that they made healthy profits and were left alone rather than dealing with the culture of illegality that was rife in the country.

A former Governor of the Central Bank, Maurice Doyle, told the committee that there were approximately one million people working in Ireland and it was his guess that about half of them knew about opening bogus non-resident accounts to avoid tax. It was, he said, so widespread that 'even the dogs in the street knew about it'.

When this was put to the former Taoiseach and Minister for Finance, Albert Reynolds, himself the founder of a pet food company in Edgeworthstown, Co Longford, he answered: 'I've a lot of respect for the dogs in the street, they're customers of mine from time to time.' But such light moments were rather rare.

At one stage an exasperated Pat Rabbitte asked the Chairman of the Central Bank: 'Can you tell me exactly what it is you do?'

The Central Bank and the Department of Finance appeared to be run by a group of well-meaning civil servants who were terrified that if they did anything about illegal deposits or upset the banks this would lead to a 'flight of capital' from the country. In other words, people would take their 'hot money' elsewhere and it would be lost to the Irish State. It became increasingly clear as the inquiry progressed that the major banks were so powerful that they were virtually untouchable. They rode roughshod over the Revenue Commissioners and ignored the Central Bank and the Department of Finance.

The hearings were held in Kildare House across the street from Leinster House. Stark and functional, the product of bad 1960s architecture, it stands in marked contrast to its surroundings: the historic National Library, Leinster House itself and the other wing of what was once the great mansion of the Duke of Kildare, the National Library. But its committee room held all the trappings of a modern inquiry, the audio-visual aids, the long circular table at which the committee sat facing the various delegations and their high-priced lawyers.

The deliberations of the committee were quick, succinct and generated huge interest among the public. The politicians proved more than a match for the delegations of bankers and businessmen who trooped through the doors of Kildare House during September and October 1999.

Mostly it was good humoured and sometimes a little tedious. But there was the occasional flash of real anger and emotion.

One such event concerned the cross-examination of Revenue witness Tony McCarthy by Dermot Gleeson SC, who was acting as legal representative for Allied Irish Banks and who was dogged in the defence of his client. Another former Attorney General, Gleeson was reputed to be the highest paid lawyer in Ireland at the time and, in imitation of Peter Sutherland, would later become a director and eventually Chairman of Allied Irish Banks.

This was a typical exchange between the two adversaries in relation to the alleged amnesty that AIB claimed McCarthy had authorised:

Gleeson: 'Look Mr McCarthy, what you said was that it was a game plan worked out from the start.'

McCarthy: 'That was my opinion.'

Gleeson: 'Yeah. So before all these records were put together of the phone calls and so on, someone said, "We will make a deceitful record of a series of phone calls." Is that what you're saying?'

McCarthy: 'This whole case has been riddled with deceit.'

Gleeson: 'No, I'm asking you a question.'

McCarthy: 'I'm answering your questions.'

Gleeson: 'Do you think, say, that somebody sat down and said: "We will fabricate a record which we'll be able to keep on our files, or internal records, which will include inaccurate notes, inaccurate statements that the board of the Revenue were involved, and we will have a spoof phone call with Mr McCarthy telling him about £2.5 million." You think that was planned in advance?'

McCarthy: 'I have no idea as to what stages it was planned, but I believe there was a game plan. In the matter of deceit, I would draw your attention to the memo of 6 September 1991 when Dr de Buitléir, the head of the department, asked me for permission to repay DIRT which was deducted by zealous bank managers on accounts wrongly designated or reclassified. He was refused. What Dr de Buitléir failed to tell me is that that was already what he was doing and that's what he continued to do. So, if you want to talk about deceit I can give you plenty of instances, Mr Gleeson.'

Chapter 18

The Customer Is Always Right

There are moments when the pure irony of a situation is lost on most people – but not everybody.

Mark Hely-Hutchinson, the younger son of the Earl of Donaghmore, had been Chief Executive of the Bank of Ireland from 1983 to 1990 and had also been Chief Executive of the world-famous Guinness brewery in Dublin for a time. The family had long links with the business establishment in Dublin and London and it was no surprise when this scion of the Protestant ascendancy took over the running of the bank, whose original headquarters was the imposing old Irish parliament in College Green, Dublin.

Tall and thin with an accent polished at Oxford, Hely-Hutchinson was slightly ill-at-ease at being called before an Irish government commission of inquiry into his stewardship of the establishment bank. But the irony was that his inquisitor, the Chairman of the inquiry, Jim Mitchell TD, a Christian Brothers' boy from a working class estate in Drimnagh, Dublin, had started his working life as a lowly office clerk in a Dickensian office in the Guinness Brewery at a time when Hely-Hutchinson was running the vast brewing enterprise.

'But I mean,' inquired Mitchell in cross-examining Hely-Hutchinson, 'there has been a very clear statement – there is a mission statement from Bank of Ireland which talks about integrity and high standards. I was just interested to know what practical steps were taken to ensure compliance on the ground with management instructions.'

Looking slightly uncomfortable, as if such chores were beneath him, Hely-Hutchinson didn't quite answer the question. So Mitchell pursued it.

'But I mean, you've experience of other industries, other business. I mean would that have been your attitude in your previous incarnation in the brewing industry?' he asked.

'You don't really want to get into the beer business, Chairman, despite your past and so on,' replied the lordly Hely-Hutchinson dismissively.

It was a put-down that wasn't lost on the small few at the parliamentary hearing who were keen students of past history and the intertwining of business, politics, education, the old order and the new republic.

What emerged from Hely-Hutchinson's evidence was that while Bank of Ireland adopted a high moral tone, they were only paying lip service at the top to the legislation governing non-resident accounts. The same executives were turning a blind eye to what was happening on the ground in the towns and villages of

Ireland. In the end, Jim Mitchell's committee proved that for all their fine talk, the Bank of Ireland guys could get down and dirty with the rest of them when it came to creaming off lucrative bank accounts for tax-dodging customers.

At the top, the members of 'The Court', as the board of directors of the bank grandly style themselves, claimed that the more they imposed the rules on their managers and officials around the country, the more they lost business to, well, less reputable institutions like Allied Irish Banks and the 'chronic ags' in ACC.

'I have a record of a discussion with the Chairman of the Revenue Commissioners in which he told me – because we were pressuring him, we having done a unilateral code of conduct of our own, we were trying to pressure the Revenue Commissioners to make sure that other banks were made to do the same thing. The record I have of the discussion with the Chairman of the Revenue Commissioners was that they weren't having much joy,' whinged Hely-Hutchinson.

The way Bank of Ireland looked at it, although Hely-Hutchinson was too polite to put it in such terms, was that it had to compete with riff-raff.

'You will understand,' he said, 'that there are two competing thrusts on a bank branch. The branch primarily exists to serve its customers. Its customers are well educated people, they are not mugs. They know what is going on in other banks. When they come in, if they want to break the law, they will know what they want to do.'

But there were other factors: 'I mean a manager would only

decide to ignore the directions of head office because of the competitive pressures and because his performance as a branch manager was going to be rated by his success in getting new deposits, so he's got two pressures against him.

'One is to obey the rules and the other is to make his own performance look good by getting in lots of deposits and you get lots of deposits if you can find a way round the rules,' said the former Chairman of Bank of Ireland, spelling out the realities of life in the small towns of Ireland in the 1980s and 1990s.

So everybody was to blame for the situation where they were cheating on taxes except 'The Court' and the executive floor in the bank's ugly headquarters in Baggot Street. There was another dodge that went into the annals of folklore in the late 1980s as the creative people of Claremorris, Co Mayo, found their own way around the situation. People with accounts in the Bank of Ireland who clearly lived in Claremorris began to open new non-resident accounts with false addresses abroad. When it was pointed out to them that this was obviously illegal they quickly found a way around it. They gave themselves new identities by using the Irish version of their names.

Like all good scams it soon got around that if you came up with an Irish version of your name and a foreign address you could beat the system.

Suddenly the practice of using Irish names began to spread. Branches of Bank of Ireland in Boyle, Athy, Killorglin, Skibbereen, Blanchardstown, Roscommon all began to get a rush of Irish-speaking depositors. It seemed such a coincidence.

'And what is your own name *as gaeilge*?' Mitchell jokingly

asked Hely-Hutchinson.

'Don't ask me,' answered the son of an Earl, who as a small boy lived in the grandeur of Knocklofty House in Co Tipperary and had obviously grown up in the public school system in England rather than with the local Christian Brothers.

But many managers and staff of the Bank of Ireland believed that if they were going to compete and hold on to business, they had to go into the bogus accounts with the same gusto as Allied Irish Banks.

Meanwhile, Mark Hely-Hutchinson and his top executives were going for nice lunches with the head of the Central Bank, the Chairman of the Revenue Commissioners, the Secretary of the Department of Finance and other influential figures where they would drone on about their grand code of conduct and complain about what was going on and how it wasn't a 'level playing field'.

'Do you ever recall getting any meaningful response?' asked Jim Mitchell.

'Oh, it would have been a very, sort of, warm polite response: what a pity these other people don't have the same ethics as you do. But the Central Bank simply didn't see it and it wasn't, within the legislation, within its function to police these things,' he replied.

Other executives were less circumspect. After a meeting between executives of Bank of Ireland and Revenue, the reality of what was going on emerged.

'While admitting irregularities at the branch, it [Bank of Ireland] wished to have it placed on record that they were encountering severe difficulties in the Munster area and particularly in Tipperary from other financial institutions of which AIB and ACC were the main culprits,' wrote Tony 'The Boot' McCarthy in a 1990 memo about how the banks were upstaging one another.

In its first report, the Parliamentary Inquiry into DIRT found that despite its 'culture of weighty responsibility, duty and ethical behaviour' some of the most celebrated cases of tax evasion took place in Bank of Ireland.

They were listed as the famous Milltown Malbay episode, while other noteworthy episodes occurred in Thurles, Boyle, Roscrea, Dundalk, Mullingar, Skibbereen and Dungarvan.

'Certainly the evidence suggests that the bank failed to successfully balance competitive need with the duty of compliance,' said the report.

The problem of holding on to customers in the cut-throat climate was also obvious in the Midland & Western Building Society, a small building society in Main Street, Longford, which was run by a couple of local businessmen who were watching their customers disappearing down the main street to institutions where they could open accounts with addresses that everybody knew were false. These were simple country businessmen and they decided that somebody should do something about it.

So they sent a letter to the Central Bank complaining about the main banks, the AIB, the ACC, Bank of Ireland, Ulster Bank and National Irish Bank. In particular, the letter alleged that the basis on which Form F was used bordered on the irresponsible. The letter alleged that substantial sums of money were being transferred into external Irish Pound accounts and that English addresses were literally being supplied to order. But there was no danger that anything would be done about it.

The Central Bank passed the letter to the Department of Finance who simply filed it away. A senior civil servant was delegated to write back an official letter saying that the problem was not 'widespread' and the Department was, of course, keeping a close eye on things.

The Minister for Finance, Ray MacSharry, in his 1987 Budget speech said, 'There appears to be some misconception about the tax status of non-resident deposits. Let me make the position clear. Such deposits are entirely free of retention tax in our jurisdiction. I can give assurances that we have no intention of changing these arrangements. Non-residents can lodge deposits here in complete confidence.'

Of course 'non-residents' didn't have to pay tax, but the clear message that was taken from such assurances, whether MacSharry intended it or not, was that anybody claiming such status could feel secure that they would never come under the scrutiny of the authorities.

But probably the most acute abusers of the system were over at the ACC, the State bank where, as late as 1993, the Internal Audit Manager, John Roche, was complaining of the 'state of disarray' with regard to bank documentation and that branch managers were openly flouting bank policy with written assurances which, he said, were 'materially untrue'. Even the staff were opening bogus non-resident accounts, using false names and addresses. Senior management withheld vital information from the board of the bank and 'consistently ignored' directives from the top.

When the government decided to sell the bank it commissioned a report into its finances from external auditors, Ernst & Young. The first draft of this report found that there was a potential liability in unpaid DIRT tax of over IR£17.5 million in 1992. Because of changes in government, the privatisation of ACC never went ahead and the top executives in the bank simply sat on the information, ignored it and never paid the tax to the government.

'I think myself that following the conversation with Mr [Billy] Moore, the Deputy Chief Executive, it was quite obvious to both of us that it was not really a really big issue at all,' said John McCloskey, the former Chief Executive of the bank referring to the unpaid taxes.

When signing off the company accounts for the year, the bank's auditors, who had come up with the calculation of IR£17.5 million, blithely signed away without making any provision in the accounts for a tax settlement. Again, like AIB, it based its decision on a 'good meeting' with Revenue who weren't told about the multi-million pound liability and so didn't ask about it.

'I mean, the judgement I made, Chairman, was made on the information that was available to me at the time,' explained John Hogan, the external auditor who worked for Ernst & Young.

Originally a farmers' bank called the Agricultural Credit Corporation, the ACC was actually owned by the State. It was far and away the worst offender among the larger financial institutions when it came to bogus non-resident accounts. Maybe it was the culture of the bank or maybe it was the more widespread aversion to paying taxes that was to be found generally in the farming community.

'The state of disarray which existed with the declarations, the failure of branches to comply with direct instructions on the issue [of DIRT] and the fact that written assurances by branch managers in December 1992 were found to be materially untrue were indicative of an attitude to banking standards and to legal requirements which needed to be sharply reversed,' said the bank's own external auditor, John Roche.

What intrigued Deputy Pat Rabbitte during the Public Account Hearings into DIRT was that although this was a huge problem throughout the banking sector, there wasn't one letter on the subject containing the name of John McCloskey, the Chief Executive of ACC.

ACC went even further than most of the other banks in that some of their staff held bogus non-resident accounts in the bank. A report on the Tullamore branch in Co Offaly read:

> Investigations at the branch revealed that a member of staff had been operating non-resident accounts with fictitious names and false addresses. These accounts were found to have been operated with the knowledge of the branch manager and assistant manager.

Yet despite this appalling behaviour, nobody seemed to want to do anything to clean up the bank. The Chairman of ACC, the politically appointed Dan McGing, explained that maybe the banking controls were not as good as they should be because, being an agricultural bank, the managers were agricultural graduates rather than bankers and business graduates.

'They were local people and they were prominent people locally. They were brought in because of their contacts in local communities and things like they . . . they were good footballers, they were hurlers,' he said.

To be fair to him, the bank was in bad shape and losing huge sums of money when he was brought in to try to turn it around. The idea of a bank losing money seemed normal enough in the Soviet style semi-State sector in Ireland in those pre-privatisation days when everything from sugar production to transport was controlled by the State.

The reason for this dismal state of affairs was that the ACC gave out a vast amount of money in loans to farmers who wouldn't repay the money back. The result was that McGing was desperately trying to 're-position' the bank in the hope that when it was in a healthier state the State could sell it off. But the board of the bank, he explained, could not go out and enforce the legislation that was being flouted by its managers.

'If that sounds sinister, it's not meant to be sinister. It means that the board couldn't go out and do it itself,' he said.

But Pat Rabbitte was not impressed with McGing's contention that the board of ACC would not tolerate bogus accounts: 'Can we clear up the little point for a start, though, of how it is you can claim that the board didn't know and you didn't know? I mean there are several examples – here's 16 March 1993 landed on your own desk, a document like this [claiming 40 per cent of non-resident documentation was unreliable] would cause the hair to stand up if I were in your position. How could you claim not to know?'

McGing could not answer the question, all he could do was reiterate that he was not aware of what was going on in the bank. But the Chief Executive, John McCloskey, knew that if they could get the depositors in and build up the bank, it could become a very valuable business.

'I remember saying to the Chief Executive that we were beginning to look at privatisation,' recalled Albert Reynolds, who was then Minister for Finance. 'But he said to me, "Look it wouldn't be worth IR£20 million today. Leave me three years and I will get you IR£100 million."'

'At the time you bore political responsibility for the bank. Is there anything you would like to say about that?' committee barrister Frank Clark SC asked Albert Reynolds.

'Oh, I wouldn't condone tax evasion in any shape or form in relation to it, and most certainly not in relation to any State institution, because it does give out the perception that, you know, the law is not there to be enforced,' said the dog food magnate who once owned a small finance company in Longford himself.

Sir George Quigley, Chairman of Ulster Bank, found the whole thing 'disappointing'. Jim Lacey, former Chief Executive of National Irish Bank, admitted that branch managers came to him and said 'they couldn't develop their deposit base unless they were going to become lax in their non-residency [regulations]'. But he insisted they were told they would be punished if they did so.

'I'm merely saying that in terms of repeating to me all of the things you tried to do to get the culture right, that here we have an assessment six years after you became Chief Executive and it found a fairly lamentable performance in terms of compliance,' countered Pat Rabbitte. Again Lacey denied that he was aware of what was going on in the branches around the country.

Alex Spain, a well-known Dublin businessman and Chairman of National Irish Bank, had to admit that a document written within the bank was 'very puzzling and one might take the wrong connotation out of it'.

This internal document read: 'We understand that a number of other NIB group banks are sending major non-resident accounts offshore to reduce documentation risks. We should consider doing likewise for major non-resident accounts.'

Pat Rabbitte wanted to know how the Chairman of the bank felt when there was a sudden 'remarkable' increase in non-resident accounts. 'What I'm trying to get at, Mr Spain, is that the evidence speaks for itself by which you meant that the bank had a good compliance record. Now the difficulty the committee is having is that we have all these documents which showed up 40 per cent of deficient declarations and so on. And it's difficult to reconcile the two positions. Do you accept that that's a fair problem on our side of the table?'

'I see it as a problem,' agreed Spain.

Another financial institution which found a way out of the

morass when they began closing up bogus non-resident accounts in the early 1990s was Irish Life & Permanent. It opened up a branch in the Isle of Man which promised 'secrecy and discretion' of the highest order. Customers were blatantly told that their money would be safe from the prying eyes of the Revenue Commissioners.

Customers who might inquire about doing business with the Isle of Man branch could not be referred on by their local branch of the IL&P, or at least that is what they would have us believe.

'If I went into the bank and said: "Listen I want to open a bank account in the Isle of Man in the Irish Permanent," and the manager said to me, "Well I can't do it for you because it would be reportable [to the Revenue] but here's the card of the man in the Isle of Man, you can telephone him yourself," would that be reportable?' asked Sean Ardagh TD at the DIRT hearings.

'My knowledge of that situation would be that it would not be reportable, that the manager could give the Isle of Man number to a customer. He could advise the customer to get in direct contact with the Isle of Man,' replied Roy Douglas, Chief Executive.

He went on to tell the Committee of Public Accounts that he would not know anything of the business transacted by his bank in the Isle of Man.

'No, I wouldn't be aware of any of the customers of the Isle of Man and there would be – under Isle of Man banking law there would be strict confidentiality requirements in place in relation to that.'

'Right, so do you know the number and value of accounts in

the Isle of Man bank held by Irish residents?'

'I have no knowledge of that whatsoever,' said Roy Douglas.

'And you have never asked, you never inquired into it?'

'Never,' answered the Chief Executive.

The Killarney Branch of the Irish Permanent was 'a particular area of concern' because, oddly enough, there was a high percentage of account holders with addresses in the United States. 'Virtually all the non-resident customers were "no correspondence" so direct contact with the customer was not possible. However, US telephone books showed a person, with the non-resident account holder's surname, living at the address recorded on the bank's record,' revealed the Comptroller and Auditor General.

Internal Audit concluded that accounts were being opened on behalf of customers using false names at an address of a relative with that surname in the US. When they couldn't come up with a relative, 'American telephone books were also used to obtain false addresses' and the accounts were marked 'no correspondence'.

The manager of the Killarney branch would later claim in court documents that he and other managers were given incentives at seminars organised by the bank to 'cherry pick' valuable customers and move their money offshore. He also claimed that he and other successful managers were paid large bonuses for attracting such business to the bank. The real value of a bogus non-resident account was that they usually involved large sums of money, which the customer was putting on deposit for a long time and so there was little or no work involved, and also they were paid a smaller rate of interest. But most importantly of all, they attracted 'Key Business Influencers' or KBIs as they were called in the bank.

KBIs were people with money and they lured others to a bank because they did their business there, a fact that was noted in the golf club bar and other social gatherings. It was a strategy that had enabled Allied Irish Banks to overtake its great rival, Bank of Ireland, as the biggest fish in the pond – a fact that was not lost on all the other creatures looking for a slice of the action in the murky world of low finance.

Chapter 19

Drama at the Hearings

When he walked into Kildare House in the centre of Dublin on the morning of Tuesday, 28 September 1999, Anthony Spollen was dapperly dressed as usual. He wore a navy suit, white shirt, a red polka dot tie, with his thick wavy hair combed back from his forehead and a briefcase swinging gently in his left hand.

He could have been any ordinary businessman going into a meeting in a modern office block, even if it was only a few steps from the front entrance to Dáil Éireann and around the corner from the United Service Club where he took his lunch most days. But on this particular occasion Anthony Spollen's features were drawn and there was a tiredness about his eyes from having been up most of the previous night, agonising over the words he would utter in the public forum he was entering.

This was important for him. He had to respond to the picture of him painted by his former boss the previous afternoon.

And he had to respond to earlier allegations, before the

Parliamentary Inquiry began, when the Chief Executive of AIB, Tom Mulcahy, had gone before a public hearing and mocked his calculations and the independent stand he had taken to defend his good name and the good name and reputation of the bank where he had worked for so long. Anthony Spollen was going to break the habit of a lifetime and speak frankly and publicly.

Ranged around the large conference room he entered were some of the biggest names in Irish business. These were men with whom he had once done business. But more than that, these were men with whom he had once been friends, men he had mingled with at social occasions in gentlemen's clubs and golf clubs and Stock Exchange dinners. Now, sitting across from him they were accompanied by a battery of high priced lawyers that only a major bank could afford. Their eyes no longer met.

Anthony Spollen was virtually all alone. Unlikely as it seemed, the banker and consultant, the man who knew most of the biggest names in business around the city was now an outsider among the people he had spent a lifetime of service with. Running through his thoughts were the words that had been teased from his former boss, Gerry Scanlan, the previous afternoon during cross-examination by Sean Doherty.

'Was Mr Spollen aggrieved by his treatment by the bank?' asked Doherty.

'He was,' agreed Scanlan.

'Was his calculation of £100 million liability "fiction"?'

'It was,' agreed Scanlan.

'Was his behaviour "childish"?'

'It was,' agreed Scanlan.

'It is a back of beyond calculation and not one on which I, as Chief Executive, would form a value judgement,' answered Scanlan, dismissing out of hand the lifetime of endeavour that Spollen had undertaken to protect the integrity of his job and the reputation of the bank which meant so much to him.

Scanlan went on to say that the corporate battle which had culminated with Spollen's departure eight years before could only have one outcome.

'It was either his job or mine,' he said.

Spollen, the company man, was deeply wounded and offended by this characterisation of him and his position as Internal Auditor of the bank. He had given loyal and dedicated service over 22 years and he was now deeply distressed to be portrayed as some sort of rogue executive who was contemplating a wrongful dismissal case against the bank that would lead to humiliating legal proceedings in the Four Courts in Dublin.

As he began to speak, his words, at first, were stuttered and slightly confused, as if there was too much emotion for one man to bear. But then he got into his stride and the men and women sitting around the horseshoe-shaped conference table listened in rapt silence.

'I have been painted by some as somebody who is a bit . . . a disgruntled guy . . . a chip on his shoulder . . . whose calculations have been called into question . . . "he was out to cause trouble".

'Nothing could be further from the truth.

'The reasons I didn't speak on this yesterday or seek to respond was I felt a little bit emotional because, for one reason, as you know, my wife hasn't been well. She would have been watching Mr Scanlan on the television and it's very hard when you're sitting there in a great deal of pain, seeing your husband being pilloried the way I was by Mr Scanlan yesterday. The subject . . . what I think Mr Scanlan didn't tell you . . . Let me tell you what he did tell you from my few notes. Forgive me if I am just a little bit all over the place.

'He said he found out in 1999 that there was a major problem with bogus accounts – 1999, long after everybody in this room heard about it, long after everybody out on the street heard about it. He heard about it in 1999.

'You've got to make up your own mind whether that's credible or not. He then produced letters that he had written to me but hadn't sent to me, years after the event. He then talked about the tax inspector, Mr McCarthy, doing some sort of an amnesty or arrangement at a football match. That may seem funny and smart and slick. I would just ask you to bear that in mind.

'He then came down to, I suppose, the nub of it all; he said, "It was either him or me." I didn't see it in that light. I was simply trying to do my job in an ordinary, decent way. I suppose that I found the cheapest, the cheapest shot of all was to suggest that Tony Spollen felt there was some kind of conspiracy theory by all the management of the bank against him.

'Nothing could be further from the truth. Over my years in the job and when I left the bank I kept my counsel. I didn't speak to anybody in terms of the matters. My great friend, Niall Crowley, who died last year . . . he never knew why I left AIB. He was my great friend, my mentor. All my oldest friends often wondered . . . and when I saw my package being printed in the newspaper, my severance package, and my kids saying, "What is this all about?" That wasn't easy.

'For me, I suppose, in all our lives there's probably a few defining moments and, I suppose, when I contrast . . . For me what's terribly important in life is decency, a bit of respect for people and when I saw, last October, Mr Mulcahy coming into a forum with some of his more junior men and making these scurrilous remarks about me, here he was suggesting that everybody else is to blame, blame all the other banks, blame Tony, blame everybody in sight.

'Contrast that with my wife when she got her cancer at the beginning of last year. She didn't blame the environment, she didn't blame anybody, she didn't blame the doctor who came and gave her the bad news. She didn't blame the person who told her of the awful treatment she was going to have to go through. She carried it with dignity and she's sitting at home, probably watching this thing now.

'At the beginning I acknowledged her courage and support. There were times when, you know, I think, men somehow when we're out there, we can take a lot, we can take a lot of abuse and that's okay. But, I think, for a wife who's out there defenceless, watching a thing, it can be very, very tough going.

'The issue I suppose, which really drew the line, I suppose for myself and Mr Scanlan – and I hate having to go through this – was a failed share issue in AIB and underwriting. It went badly wrong and rather than face the music and admit it, the bank had been left with an underwriting stick [loss]. What happened was the shares were put into the Widows' and Orphans' account, into the staff pension fund account. The whole thing . . . the Stock Exchange was never informed . . .'

At this point in his reverie, Spollen was interrupted by the eminent barrister Dermot Gleeson SC who could no longer contain himself. He was representing Allied Irish Banks and defending the performance and integrity of the executives whose actions Spollen was now calling into question. But now his balancing act was being severely tried – on the one hand he did not want to antagonise Spollen further, but he certainly wasn't going to let him go down the road of opening up another can of worms. He had to put the lid on the emotional outburst that had taken everybody by surprise.

After Dermot Gleeson's interruption, Spollen made an attempt to re-start his diatribe. 'I want, I didn't interrupt anybody else,' he countered.

But Gleeson was determined not to let this emotional outburst continue: 'I don't want to add at all to Mr Spollen's distress, I really don't and I can see that he is distressed. I certainly don't wish to interfere with any rights of speech that he may have here, but it is my duty, unhappily at the moment, because of the distress which he is in, to draw to your attention that the matters upon which he is now elaborating are matters upon which I have no instruction.'

He was referring to the 'Dana Affair' and the other alleged malpractices which Anthony Spollen had set out in his papers, 'The Facts' and 'Octopus'. These were outside the terms of reference of the Dáil inquiry and Gleeson certainly didn't want them aired at a public forum that was being televised live. With his interruption the moment of emotion had passed.

What had driven Spollen's outburst, and finally led to the schism that showed the bankers in their true colours for the first time, had been the teasing cross-examination of Gerry Scanlan by Sean Doherty TD, the former detective. Doherty was often referred to in the media as the 'disgraced' ex-Minister for Justice in Charlie Haughey's government because he had been sacked for illegally tapping the telephones of several well-known journalists in order to try to trap a mole in the cabinet who was feeding the journalists information.

Doherty was sharp and had lost none of his old police training. While the other bankers and their legal advisors were being careful and measured in their answers, it took Doherty to expose the ill-feeling that Gerry Scanlan still felt for the Internal Auditor who had caused him so much trouble all those years before.

Jim Mitchell, the Chairman of the inquiry, was also in a dilemma. He wanted to hear Spollen's fascinating insight, but he was also compromised by the rules of the committee which did not allow the inquiry to stray into the secret world of the internal politics of AIB where it had all started so long ago.

'I think we have allowed Mr Spollen an opportunity to say a few words,' said Mitchell.

'Could I just conclude . . . All I want to say is – I suppose really what started – you could sense probably from yesterday's meeting that the relationship between Mr Scanlan, who I'd say was a good Chief Executive, was a little bit fraught. There was no doubt about that. Having said that, it all arose because one time he wanted me to change and audit a report which I refused . . .'

But Jim Mitchell was firm. 'No, no maybe we shouldn't go into that today.'

Anthony Spollen wasn't finished.

'Chairman, can I just say I hope . . . and I thank you. I am terribly sorry to have had to say what I have had to say . . . I sat up all night thinking about it last night and were it not for . . . I tried to behave decently and when I saw Mr Scanlan's performance yesterday, it was just the straw that broke the camel's back. I am sorry . . .'

Then the moment passed and they moved on and that rare insight into the emotional lives of bankers was filed away. That lunchtime they all trooped out of Kildare House and around the corner and up the steps of the United Service Club where they dined at separate tables.

Chapter 20

Bringing Home the Bacon

'Tell me, who do you think brought home the bacon?' asked Pat Rabbitte TD.

'What bacon?' replied Gerry Scanlan, slightly mystified by this unusual question.

'The deal?' asked Rabbitte, a skilled politician and a man who would eventually go on to lead the Irish Labour Party.

'I would guess both Jimmy O'Mahony and Dr de Buitléir and I'm pretty confident that's who it was – both ex-Revenue men,' answered Scanlan, making the not-so-subtle point that the brightest and the best from the office of the Revenue Commissioners eventually ended up working in the banks. One move to the private sector and they could double their salaries with pay, perks and valuable share options.

'You don't know who was on the other side of the deal?' asked Rabbitte.

'No.'

'It certainly wasn't Mr McCarthy I think,' said Rabbitte, by way of a rhetorical question, referring to the taxman. McCarthy's meeting in 1991 with senior officials of AIB was the basis for the bank's belief in an amnesty from unpaid taxes if it quickly 'got its house in order' and ended the widespread use of bogus non-resident accounts in the banking system.

'No, I don't think so. Mr McCarthy is the affable man down there at the end of the table,' said Scanlan, pointing down at the taxman.

Scanlan, the former Chief Executive of Allied Irish Banks, was a man not used to being cross-examined, especially by someone like Pat Rabbitte who might be regarded, in his political life, as unfriendly to banks and bankers.

'My God, there wasn't anything affable about the evidence he gave this committee a couple of weeks ago when it came to AIB. He had a very definite line on AIB,' said Rabbitte.

McCarthy's barb that 'he didn't go to the AIB school of languages' had been a clear reference to his belief that they had twisted his words in order to concoct a deal, a deal he maintained he had never agreed. He said he had never given them the amnesty to which they were now clinging desperately.

He also disputed the words of the bank's senior tax advisor, Jimmy O'Mahony, who claimed that on 5 March 1991 McCarthy had told him that the amnesty had the 'approval of The Castle', meaning it was sanctioned by the board of the Revenue Commissioners. McCarthy said that the evidence presented by Allied Irish Banks had been 'riddled with deceit'.

Scanlan listened to this long list of unfavourable comments

about the bank where he had been boss and which had made him a very wealthy man.

'Well, he seems to have been able to have social occasions with some of our senior people at the same time, either at football matches or otherwise,' replied Scanlan, dropping his little bombshell without much diplomacy into the midst of the proceedings which to that moment had been more concerned with official matters and boardroom confrontations.

What was he saying? Was there a cosy relationship between the Revenue Commissioners and the tax advisors to the major banks? After all, they were all tax experts. Many of them met together for business at the Institute of Taxation and enjoyed a convivial glass of wine afterwards. Many of them had also been colleagues together in the Revenue Commissioners at various times, before some of them moved on to the more lucrative pastures of the banking industry. Poacher turned gamekeeper sprung to mind.

Certainly it occurred to the sharp mind of the Chairman, Jim Mitchell. He pounced.

'Would you elaborate on that?' he asked.

Scanlan was only too willing to take the bait. 'Yes, Chairman. If you refer to a question of informal meetings, my understanding was that Pat O'Mahony [Head of Branches at Allied Irish Banks], who was the person involved, met Mr McCarthy at a GAA match. Now, whether it's right or wrong, I don't know, but that's what my colleagues have mentioned to me as a likelihood.'

Rabbitte: 'And the deal was done in Croke Park?'

Scanlan: 'Well, I guess Cork were playing wherever the deal

was done.'

This was a reference to the fact that both O'Mahony and McCarthy came from the Cork town of Bandon, where they had attended the same school many years before.

Rabbitte: 'So you think this deal was done at a GAA match in Cork?'

Scanlan: 'No, I did not say that, Deputy. A deal would appear to have been done between the Revenue people and Dr de Buitléir and Jimmy O'Mahony, possibly at Bankcentre, some Dublin location I would say is most likely anyhow . . . and I would say it was a working location.'

'Ok,' said Rabbitte, 'So, as far as you were concerned, you had an amnesty?'

'Amnesty is the word that's used in the documentation,' replied Scanlan. 'I understood that there were discussions going on between our tax people and the Revenue which resulted in an agreement which, as I detected at the time, people in the bank felt happy about and that essentially this enormous blooming problem that we had was going to . . . we had an environment developing in which it would be resolved.'

For Jim Mitchell and the other politicians investigating AIB, the idea that the Revenue Commissioners could have contemplated 'a deal' was, as Lord Denning so aptly put it in another context, 'an appalling vista'.

The basic facts are that after the meeting on 13 February 1991 between Allied Irish Banks and the Revenue Commissioners, two things happened. Allied Irish Banks agreed to pay IR£14 million in uncollected DIRT tax, and kept paying more in subsequent years, and the Revenue Commissioners walked away from the bank and the issue of bogus non-resident accounts.

They never uttered another word about it. They never went through with the proposed Revenue Paper on the problem of DIRT. They ignored dire warnings which were passed on to them via the Department of Finance from disgruntled competitors who were finding their customers disappearing into the open arms of AIB and ACC. They never lifted a finger to go in and investigate Allied Irish Banks until seven years later when the full story appeared in the *Sunday Independent*. And even then, they appear to have done their best to ignore it.

Dr Donal de Buitléir, the head of the tax section of Allied Irish Banks, told his colleagues at the time: 'As you know, at a meeting with the Investigation Branch of the Revenue Commissioners on 13 February [1991] . . . the question of general compliance with the retention tax provisions was raised. At the meeting the Revenue Commissioners accepted that a determined effort was being made to ensure that all non-resident accounts exempted from retention tax were genuine. They now wish to provide the AIB, together with all other financial institutions, an opportunity to put their house in order with no retrospection prior to 5 April 1990.'

The matter was raised at the board of Allied Irish Banks, who decided that because they were now 'forward looking' they had escaped a huge potential liability.

The man who had been investigating the bank's use of bogus non-resident accounts, Tony McCarthy, was suddenly given other duties to attend to.

'My recollection about the time is that there was a sudden breakthrough – for want of a better word – in the drinks industry which gave us tentacles into a huge number of pubs because of certain information we had about the actual distribution of drink and that there were very significant yields and Mr McCarthy was one of the most experienced officers and he moved to head that project up – "Scorpion",' conceded Sean Moriarty, McCarthy's boss at the Revenue Commissioners.

Lochlann Quinn, the businessman who succeeded Peter Sutherland as Chairman of Allied Irish Banks had a more blunt view. Revenue, he maintained stoutly, 'walked away' from the issue.

'But it is clear to me, at that particular stage, taking the detailed contemporaneous notes of our own staff, followed by the Revenue's behaviour . . . I mean, they walked away. I mean it wasn't a case that they walked away not knowing the figures were there. When you have a substantial leap in DIRT payment in the next six months and the six months after that, it's clear you have a historic problem . . . Well, it's quite clear the Revenue knew they had cleaned up the situation with AIB,' stated Quinn.

'It's odd, isn't it?' asked Pat Rabbitte, 'It's funny that the Revenue wouldn't bother to come and collect it?' he said.

'Well, I think it's consistent with the fact that we had a deal. Their behaviour is consistent with – that we had a deal,' answered Lochlann Quinn.

Dr Donal de Buitléir, who was head of Group Taxation at AIB, was in no doubt either: 'I attended the meeting of 6 September 1991 in place of Mr O'Mahony, who was ill. At that meeting I was left in no doubt that Mr McCarthy was gratified by our response to his initiative and that there were no outstanding issues on his side.'

According to Jimmy O'Mahony, who like de Buitléir had worked in the Revenue before they were headhunted by Allied Irish Banks, there was also a deal. O'Mahony, who had been Group Taxation manager before de Buitléir at AIB, went even further: 'I was firmly of the view that we had an arrangement and a forward arrangement to get this matter on stream and he [McCarthy] was going to do the same with other institutions.

'It was a forward going arrangement which we had. This was discussed at that meeting, the letter from the Inspector and subsequent telephone conversations which we had. I put that all together. I wasn't going to put something on the table to the bank that here was a forward arrangement, there's the deal, we go and clean up the situation that's there, unless I was satisfied that that was it. Other colleagues also accepted that there was an arrangement here.

'At all times we had notes of our meeting on 13 February. We then get the Inspector's letter. We disagree with a certain amount of the content. We go back to Mr McCarthy and we discuss it on the phone. That is my understanding of what was discussed on the phone. I would have no reason to put that in writing, bring it to the bank and say, "We have a deal," unless I was sure of my ground. Other people subsequently looked at the correspondence and file notes which I had and concurred with that view.'

But the one word that nobody got in writing was 'amnesty' and this was a matter of vital importance to both sides.

'I don't believe the Revenue could have put it in writing that they were writing off taxes. Far from being a "rotten" bank, as one member of the DIRT committee called it, Allied Irish Banks regarded itself as above board and responsible,' maintained Jimmy O'Mahony.

It was the same story from the former Chairman of Allied Irish Banks, Peter Sutherland: 'I was certainly satisfied that there was an agreement.'

The only dissenting voice from Allied Irish Banks was Anthony Spollen, the Internal Auditor who took the fall. A man of propriety and high standards, he couldn't imagine such a solution being arrived at by two important corporate organisations such as a bank and the Revenue.

'I know in the real world I don't think they [the Revenue] would have countenanced agreement, not in a million years, if they'd understood the scale of the problem,' he said.

The notion that AIB was 'sorting things out' as had been conveyed to Tony McCarthy didn't wash with him either.

'That's wrong,' Spollen said.

But Spollen's old friend Peter Sutherland was sure that there was an agreement and that the problem was being sorted out.

Why? Well the Audit Committee of AIB were all very important men and if they were satisfied, so was Peter Sutherland.

'Above all, in the first instance, the Audit Committee [of the bank] was satisfied that there was an agreement. They were satisfied and I should point out that they . . . you've already been given the names, I think, of the Audit Committee, but one of them was Sir Douglas Morpeth who's been president of the chartered accountants in Britain, and I think also our auditors signed off on the situation, so I was quite satisfied at the end of this process that the agreement was, and the board was as a whole.'

Committee members may have been impressed by the name dropping of Sir Douglas Morpeth, but the reality was that the Audit Committee had signed off on the deal because they really wanted to believe that the bank, of which they were directors, could not suddenly be facing a tax liability of IR£100 million. Not only was it a vast sum, but it was the first they heard of it. It was such a shock to the system they couldn't believe it was there.

But their contention that there was an 'unofficial' amnesty did have a ring of truth to it.

There was only one independent witness to whether or not there was a deal and this was Maurice O'Connell, Governor of the Central Bank of Ireland and the regulator for the financial services industry.

'If there was a tax problem, AIB told us also at the same time that they were actually involved in discussions with the Revenue Commissioners to solve this problem,' he told the DIRT hearing. 'AIB rang us in March 1991; they told us that the liability was likely to be IR£5 million.'

So if AIB was telling the regulator that they had a tax problem that they wanted to settle, it must be fair to believe that they had also come to some sort of an agreement with the Revenue Commissioners. Although with AIB you never quite knew. They had, as McCarthy the taxman pointed out, their own 'school of languages'.

Their strategy during the infamous ICI debacle all those years before had been to hire a high-powered public relations executive and even import American experts to advise them on the best way to succeed in panicking the Irish government into doing exactly what they wanted. It worked; the government of Garrett FitzGerald bought the huge loss-making insurance company in the belief that the banking system in the country was about to collapse. In that, they [AIB] had succeeded admirably.

Who is to know that they didn't follow a similar strategy now? They had 15 pages of notes and they had two senior executives who would swear there was an unofficial deal. But the vital word 'amnesty' was missing, so who was to say?

As Jim Culliton told the Dáil committee investigating the whole affair, 'You are going to need the wisdom of Job to sort it out.'

For Dermot Gleeson SC, acting for the banks, it was simply a matter of logic.

'I believe that there is very powerful evidence available to you that the key to the events of 13 February were that Mr McCarthy was there acting, putting in place, test driving if you like, the ideas which dominated his thinking . . . and that the uncanny resemblance of the deal which Ms Fullen wrote down on record on 13 February and in subsequent memos to the proposals made by Mr McCarthy, to the ideas eventually proposed by Mr Moriarty, is just too much of a coincidence,' Gleeson said, summing up the bank's case.

'Part of those ideas were that you would have the Chairman of the Revenue Commissioners and the Chief Executive of the bank.

He couldn't produce those parties. He did the next best thing. He brought four senior inspectors in and asked that a bank manager come as well and those ideas took flight. The bank took his proposal, ran with it and the idea ran and stayed running until the bank had performed their obligations and the Revenue performed theirs and that arrangement continued undisturbed, without a screed of dissent from the Revenue until the furore of 1998.

'And apart from the Moriarty memorandum, there is a piece of evidence which speaks louder than any other – it's the absence of the documents in those seven years on the Revenue side. Not a document. And the explanation proffered to you by Mr McCarthy that it was, that he was busy with the drinks industry and that the file was on the floor and that he's not sure who got it after him and that, you know, maybe someday someone was going to go back to it. Well I don't know. It stretches credibility, really. I think that any inhabitant of the real world would view those facts, would reach the conclusion that the file lay on the floor because that was the destination agreed for it in the arrangement that was made.'

It was a powerful argument.

He then went on to Anthony Spollen who had started it all.

'He was,' said Gleeson, 'the only witness who made a resolute attempt to move outside his terms of reference and he did, I think, on the last occasion he gave evidence, offer an analysis of the AIB deal. And I'm compelled to observe that he gave evidence that there was no deal as it were, but that was a matter in which he was not involved and in which I think, he would not claim any particular expertise. He also, somewhat unusually, claimed, protested, his loyalty to AIB. So, I think that one would treat some of the evidence there with caution. I'll say no more than that.'

As to McCarthy, his evidence, said the barrister, 'invites disbelief on half a dozen fronts.'

But one piece of McCarthy's evidence certainly stood out. Somebody had ordered him to drop the bank investigation and start targeting the publicans in the operation named 'Scorpion'. Despite the inquiry, which lasted six weeks, nobody ever discovered who had given the orders to leave the bank files on the floor and move on to the drinks industry. But we would discover that McCarthy was very angry at the perceived slight to his reputation, particularly Scanlan's implication that he had done a deal at a football match:

'There was quite a scurrilous comment made by Mr Scanlan which I want to firmly reject . . . that I did some dealing at a match in Cork or in the Bankcentre. To put the record straight, the last time I attended Cork was in the all Ireland semi-final replay in 1983 and, whilst I had great vision as to what was going on in AIB, I don't believe I had eight years advance notice.

'With regard to Bankcentre, I think – I know – I was there once. It was after my visit to Galway [for a tax investigation on a branch of AIB]. Some weeks later I was invited by Pat O'Mahony to go there because he hadn't seen me for a considerable time. I would mention that Mr O'Mahony and I had actually been at the same school, the Hamilton High School in Bandon – he finished in '63 and I finished in '64. In the 35 years since I have seen Pat O'Mahony at most ten times, but that one visit to the Bankcentre was an education in the way I operate, because at the last moment Mr Jimmy O'Mahony joined us for a meal and at the dessert Mr O'Mahony raised the question of my visit to Galway and I'm sure he will confirm that I rounded on him very strongly and told him I didn't mix business and pleasure and two minutes later Mr O'Mahony withdrew from the table and didn't return for an hour and a half. I want to put it clearly on the record that is not the way I operate and I absolutely reject the scurrilous attempt to damage my good name and the way it has been done.'

At which point Gerald B Scanlan, the former Chief Executive of Allied Irish Banks did something that he wasn't used to doing, he apologised.

But the way he managed to get such an inference into the hearings is possibly an indication of the way a serious banker works.

Chapter 21

The Result

On the afternoon of Tuesday, 12 October 1999, I got a phone call to say that Jim Mitchell, the Chairman of the 'Parliamentary Inquiry into DIRT' was having a few drinks in Buswell's Hotel that evening to celebrate the end of the formal hearings of the DIRT committee and would I like to join him and the committee and other journalists who had an interest in its deliberations.

I hadn't attended many of the hearings, but I liked Jim Mitchell. He had been a good friend of the news editor of the *Evening Herald*, John McHale, when I started in journalism in Dublin and we'd met from time to time in Leinster House or on social occasions. It still rankled that I had been talking to him one morning and he hadn't told me that later that day he was going to release the notorious Littlejohn brothers – but I'd got over it.

When I arrived in Buswell's that evening I made my way through the throng of politicians, lawyers, committee staff and journalists to thank him for the invitation.

'You deserve it,' he answered, 'You started it all.'

Before he had wound up the six weeks of hearings at 3.10pm that afternoon, Jim Mitchell had become somewhat emotional about what had taken place.

'Many new precedents have been set by this inquiry. Indeed, it is not an exaggeration to say that history has been made and that many will study and comment on these proceedings and their genesis for a long time to come,' he said.

'Of particular significance is the fact that neither phase has been interrupted by a legal challenge of any sort. I hope this fact can be taken as a positive commentary on the painstaking preparations undertaken by the committee to ensure that the full requirements of natural and constitutional justice were met.'

Mitchell could hardly have realised how prophetic his words were – because an attempt, just two years later, to hold a similar parliamentary inquiry into the shooting of John Carty during a siege at his home in Abbeylara, in Co Longford never got off the ground as it became bogged down in legal challenges and legislative disputes.

But now, as he reflected on 26 days of public hearings, which were televised by TG4, the testimony of 142 witnesses, some of them the most important figures in Irish business, and the decision that the committee would have to take which would cost someone hundreds of millions of euro, Jim Mitchell could rightly say that the principal objectives of the committee had been met.

'It is our hope that the cause of public accountability will have been advanced by this entire process and the profession of politics and how politicians work will have been elevated to a level which meets justifiable public expectations,' he said.

He may have got a little carried away when he prophesised that televised versions of future committees, tribunals and the courts 'might replace programmes like *Home and Away* as the public's favourite television'. But it was a genuine aspiration.

At one stage I left the reception room and went into the bar of Buswell's and bumped into an old friend who had previously owned a bar in the vicinity of Baggot Street. He asked what I was doing and when I told him, he said he'd been watching the committee hearings on television with great interest.

'I knew some of those Revenue guys,' he said, 'They used to come in to me. They had targets to meet and once they met the targets then it didn't matter. I've no love for banks or bankers, but in this case I'd believe them that there was a deal.'

I went back into the reception and rejoined Jim Mitchell who was talking to another old friend, the commentator Eamon Dunphy.

'Well Collins, who do you believe?' Dunphy asked with the usual mischievous twinkle in his eye.

Fresh from the conversation I'd just had and aware that in reality if you walk away from something for seven years then it's fair to say you've given up on it, I gave my opinion that I was more inclined to believe the bankers than the civil servants. Dunphy laughed and turned the question on Mitchell.

Jim Mitchell didn't agree or disagree at that moment. After all, he had his report to write. But when it was published a few weeks later on 15 December 1999, it was clear that he and his committee did not accept that the Revenue Commissioners had walked away from the tax-dodging banks and other financial institutions.

To do so would be a sharp slap in the face to the ordinary working people of Ireland who were bled dry by the tax authorities at a time when the banks and the fat cat businessmen and the small shopkeepers were hiding their 'hot' money in bogus accounts, illegal insurance products and offshore accounts from the Isle of Man to Jersey and from the border town of Newry to the Cayman Islands.

'There was no deal, agreement or amnesty involving the write-off of tax. The fact that AIB was allowed to persuade themselves that they may have an understanding to this effect is due in part to the negligence of the Revenue Commissioners,' said the report, which is a curious paragraph in that it starts off with a definitive statement but tapers off with an explanation of why something might have been interpreted the way it was.

The report continued: 'Nothing that transpired at the meeting of 13 February 1991 between AIB and the Revenue can be construed as a deal to write off arrears of DIRT.' Of course this is true. But the nub of the question was not what transpired at the meeting, it was what transpired afterwards. The answer is nothing. The files were left on the office floor of Tony McCarthy in Nassau Street, Dublin and everybody got on with their lives until the scandal surfaced in 1998.

Had that story never been written the money would never have been collected. Now, all these years later, I still believe that Jim Mitchell and his committee got it wrong when they found that there was 'no deal'.

But the report, and a subsequent final report of the Parliamentary Inquiry into DIRT were scathing about the banks, the Revenue, the Central Bank and the Department of Finance – and, of course, about the people of Ireland, or at least that section of them who deliberately went out with the intention of not paying their taxes. After all, nobody was ever forced to tell lies or open a bogus account.

'It is now absolutely clear that the reported problem at AIB was an industry wide phenomenon, as indeed was stated by AIB at the time of the commencement of our investigations,' said the final report.

'As we approach the end of this inquiry we must say also that unconscionably, a State bank owned by the Minister for Finance of the day – the ACC – and the country's largest banking institution – AIB Group – were among the worse cases discovered by the inquiry.

'But the practice was utterly pervasive, extending down to the smallest institutions with the smallest domestic deposit-taking institutions examined – GE Woodchester, proportionately the worst offender of all.'

Now that the Revenue Commissioners was found, officially, not to have reached an amnesty it was open season on the banks, the financial institutions and ultimately their customers.

The effect on the financial institutions was probably best summed up by the colourful Michael Fingleton of the Irish Nationwide Building Society, who had cleverly courted publicity by being the only businessman who would give feckless journalists a loan to buy a house back in the 'bad old days' when none of us had money.

'There is no profit in this, it costs a huge amount of money and it costs us a huge amount of time and a huge amount of disruption,' he said of the financial institutions' love affair with bogus non-resident accounts. 'Nobody in their right sense could say that they would continue in a haphazard manner again.'

His words were seized on by the author of the final report of the Parliamentary Inquiry into DIRT, dated 3 April 2001.

'The haphazard manner of behaviour identified by Michael Fingleton was the large scale engagement of banks and building societies with many thousands of their customers in an enormous intrigue to evade tax. This was not simply an exercise in the evasion of the Deposit Interest Retention Tax, but in many cases the object was to hide from the Revenue income and wealth on which no tax had ever been paid.'

It was this last sentence which was to cause more grief, and if anecdotal evidence is to be believed, even suicide as the banks and financial institutions began to hand over the personal records of their customers to the Revenue Commissioners. Having persuaded customers to open such accounts in the first place, the banks, without compunction, not only handed over their own records, but they also began to hand over their customers' records to the Revenue Commissioners as well.

The war of attrition was on, and before it was over, the banks, the financial institutions, and most of all their once-wealthy clients, would find themselves a lot poorer as the grim reaper called the taxman collected about €1 billion in DIRT, unpaid taxes and penalties. Some people thought they could keep their heads down and hide, but in the end they were all found out as each non-resident account was painstakingly trawled.

Even those who had taken their money from bogus non-resident accounts to hide it away in safe destinations like Jersey and further afield found themselves caught in the ever-tightening net. Because these funds could only be transferred through one of the main clearing banks in Dublin, records existed of every transaction. All it took was court orders, and the Revenue Commissioners began to obtain them by the thousand so that they could examine in detail the financial affairs of people suspected of holding bogus and offshore accounts which held untaxed money.

One by one the banks began to stump up the money. AIB paid IR£34.5 million in unpaid tax – very close to its own one-time estimate. But it was also compelled to pay IR£55 million in interest and a paltry penalty of IR£388,000 because of a six year time limit on DIRT non-compliance. The total of interest, tax and penalties paid by the bank was IR£90,044,190.

The next biggest offender, as expected, was Bank of Ireland. It paid a total of IR£30.5 million.

The much smaller, State-owned ACC, which had been singled out as one of the worst offenders in the DIRT era, paid IR£17,901,100.

In total, the banks paid over IR£173 million in back taxes, fines and penalties. These were, said the Chairman of the Revenue Commissioners, 'full and final settlements for the liabilities concerned'.

But they still had to go after the customers for what they called 'the underlying tax'. This included unpaid DIRT tax, but more importantly any tax that had not been paid on that money before it was lodged in the bank.

The Revenue Commissioners then cleverly issued another semi-amnesty on 2 May 2001 for holders of bogus non-resident accounts. The banks were told to send letters informing account holders that their details were being passed to Revenue. Meanwhile, the Revenue sent out 70,000 letters telling account holders that if they came forward by October 2002 and made voluntary disclosures, the Revenue Commissioners would not 'name and shame' them, and the penalties incurred would be limited to no more than the original amount held in the account.

The amnesty ended on 15 November 2001 after 8,500 people came forward and handed over €227 million in unpaid taxes.

Then it was down to a war on tax dodgers as batches of letters, 30,000 in October 2002 and further mailshots in January and March–June 2003, were sent to account holders telling them they had been identified in court orders as holders of accounts and it was time to settle up with the tax authorities.

Ironically, it was the holders of the larger accounts who settled first. Mainly because they could afford better tax and legal advice, they were well informed and also because they were more anxious to avail of the clause that would allow them to stay anonymous.

'For some the pressure became too much. One self-employed man from the south-west committed suicide last St Stephen's Day,' reported the *Sunday Business Post*. 'His wife said he couldn't bear to see himself named and shamed.'

According to the story, a woman and her husband set up a joint account with AIB in the early 1970s. They claimed they didn't know it was a 'bogus' account until they were informed by their bank in March.

'Words cannot describe what happened at Christmas. I don't think I can ever get over the trauma, pain and grief I went through. To think that all this upset my husband so much that he felt he could not live, that he couldn't take it any more.'

But Gerard Howard of the Revenue had some stark advice to holders of accounts: 'If you have been caught, you know who you are and we have access to all your bank records. There is no way to spoof your way out of it. You should come forward and pay.'

An organisation was set up in Cork to help holders of accounts. There was talk of suing the banks for encouraging people to evade tax. But in the end the protests fizzled out under the relentless gaze of the taxman and the stoic façade of the main banking organisations who took no responsibility for their part in the scandal, apart from paying what they were forced to stump up.

After the initial rush and the slow war of attrition, the main thrust of the investigation was over in two years. Then the tax authorities turned their attention to those who had once had bogus accounts, but had moved them offshore once the banks began to clamp down on bogus accounts in 1991 and 1992.

Money that AIB had moved to the Retail Deposit Centre and that Irish Permanent had moved offshore to the Isle of Man was now widely distributed in secretive tax havens around the world.

But the international threat of money laundering as a result of the drugs trade had led to new tax treaties. Secretive destinations like the Isle of Man and Jersey were opening up to the tax authorities in the wake of international pressure.

There was also the fact that much of the money had been moved through the banks' own clearing houses in Dublin, so records existed of transactions with offshore subsidiaries and banks.

The money trail never ceases to exist. According to the Annual Report of the Revenue Commissioners for 2006, the investigation into bogus non-resident accounts was 99 per cent completed.

The banks had paid € 225 million.

People who had come forward voluntarily had paid another € 227 million.

The follow-up investigations had yielded € 397.5 million.

The total tax from holders of bogus non-resident accounts was a staggering € 849.7 million. The interest and penalties involved were almost double the tax which people paid.

The spin-off investigation into offshore assets brought in another € 852 million. Combined with the investigation launched as a result of Charlie Bird and George Lee's story on the Clerical Medical Insurance scam, the Revenue had raised more than € 2 billion as a result of financial scandals brought to its attention by the media.

And it had all started with a pint in a pub in the Dublin docks and a complaint about Dana Exploration, a long forgotten company that still exists on the London stock exchange list.

Chapter 22

A Red Ferrari and God's Banker

Lochlann Quinn, Chairman of Allied Irish Banks, drove his bright red Ferrari along the Stillorgan dual carriageway on his way home from a reception in the residence of the American Ambassador to celebrate the 4th of July, 1999. The trials and tribulations he had endured during the DIRT Inquiry were beginning to fade. The bank was on the verge of reaching an agreement with the Revenue Commissioners and he, at least, was glad to be shut of the whole sorry mess that had dogged the last two years of his stewardship of the bank.

Quinn had been rather unlucky. He was the one who had to bear the brunt of sorting out the huge problems that had presented themselves since he opened his paper that Sunday morning in 1998. It was a scandal that happened before his time and of which he had only the vaguest notion, yet he had been left 'holding the baby'.

Until that issue had raised its ugly head, there had been only one serious thorn in his side as Chairman of Ireland's most profitable bank. That was the Annual General Meeting when a coterie of dissident former employees and shareholders, led by Niall Murphy, set out to make AIB's big day as miserable as possible for the silky individuals sitting in their Armani suits at the top table. Quinn, who had a pugnacious air about him, had tackled the dissidents head-on, imposing a time limit on questioning and insisting that anybody who spoke should identify themselves and the number of shares they held in the bank. It was a tactic aimed at curbing the small but vocal minority whose criticisms invariably became the focus of the big day, rather than the good news that the bank was presenting to shareholders.

Just when he appeared to have rallied the ordinary shareholders, who were more than happy with the fat dividends and the substantial increase in the share price, the whole DIRT business had surfaced. It was an embarrassment to the bank and its directors, it intensified the animosity between the dissidents and the board and it allowed critics to call AIB a 'rotten' bank. But in the end the board always won.

Now, as Lochlann Quinn turned his sleek Italian machine into Nutley Avenue, making his way by a circuitous route towards his home in leafy Shrewsbury Road, Dublin's premier address, he found himself confronted by another situation he could not control. Having observed him driving in what was described as 'an erratic manner', Garda Brendan O'Connor stopped Quinn's car. To Quinn's considerable embarrassment, he was asked to step out of his Ferrari and 'blow into the bag'. Unfortunately, the test proved positive and he was arrested and later charged with driving while drunk with 288mg alcohol per 100ml urine.

When the matter was dealt with at Dublin District Court on 5 May 2000, Quinn (59) insisted, despite the evidence, on denying the charges.

'Those of us who take a drink have all fallen by the wayside and can readily forgive Mr Quinn because he was incapable of making a sensible decision in that condition,' said Niall Murphy, the aforementioned dissident shareholder, in a newsletter to the bank's shareholders and pensioners, referring to the fact that the Chairman had made the ill-considered decision to drive after drinking.

'However there was no excuse for Mr Quinn's sober denial of the charges with evidence of 288mg alcohol per 100ml urine against him. This unwise denial mirrors his behaviour as Chairman of AIB. Mr Quinn should have pleaded guilty, apologised and paid his fine which is precisely what we want him to do now in respect of AIB DIRT.'

In the end Quinn did exactly that, because there was no escaping the taxman and he had the ignominy, as Chairman of the bank, of personally signing off on the €90 million settlement made in back tax and penalties with the Revenue Commissioners. It was the biggest single settlement ever made between a business and the State.

Once this had been achieved, AIB and all the other financial institutions began handing over tens of thousands of their tax-dodging clients to the Revenue Commissioners. It was a long, arduous business and led to much bitterness on the part of customers who claimed that they had only got into bogus non-resident accounts because they had taken the advice of their bankers.

Yet the DIRT disaster had, in many ways, prepared Lochlann Quinn and his board for the rocky road ahead. The report of Jim Mitchell's committee in 2001 was a damning indictment of the bank. But with a combination of hard work, the best public relations advisors a bank could buy and the convincing story that they had a 'forward looking' amnesty with the Revenue, they held the line until what was called 'the furore' died down.

Nobody resigned, nobody got fired and the shareholders had hardly recovered from the hiccup when the AIB stock began to soar once more.

In February 2002, Lochlann Quinn and Allied Irish Banks were back in the unwelcome glare of the international limelight after it was revealed that rogue trader John Rusnak had lost a staggering €691 million of the bank's money playing the currency markets – and losing on a grand scale over a long period of time.

Rusnak was a currency trader in the US subsidiary First Maryland and his stupendous gift for losing money had gone unnoticed by his bosses in America and in Ireland long enough for him to become one of the biggest losers in the history of international finance, rivalled in recent history only by Nick Leeson, the man notorious for bringing down Barings Bank with losses of almost US$1.5 billion. How Rusnak covered it up for so long was a mystery.

Observers were also shocked that a bank the size of AIB could stagger from one disaster to another. They were baffled by the ICI debacle, followed by the DIRT disaster and now here was another scandal of international proportions playing itself out in public. Once again the top management stayed intact. Maybe they're just tougher on the fourth floor of Bankcentre than most other business organisations. But, of course, Irish politicians and businesspeople are famous for their resolution in the face of disaster. They never resign. They cling to the wreckage until eventually everything is all right again – and their meek shareholders never lose a dividend.

'It's like looking at a road accident happening in front of you in slow motion,' said Quinn later. 'Immediately after that you have a problem to deal with and you get so immersed in dealing with it and taking decisions that there is only a tiny part of your brain ticking away saying: "Why did this happen?"'

Of course a little drink driving case and a two-year suspension from driving wasn't a big deal with a chauffeur-driven Mercedes provided as a perk for the Chairman of AIB. But he would probably have preferred it never happened, in the same way that he would have preferred never to have heard of DIRT or a trader called John Rusnack. But when a man is in charge of a multi-national like Glen Dimplex, has a share in the trendy Merrion Hotel in Dublin and even owns his own 118-acre French vineyard, Chateau de Fieuzal (which he bought at a cost of €45 million), it is a slight setback not to be able to take one's Ferrari for a jaunt along the byroads of south Dublin, even if the speed limit rarely exceeds 80kph. We all like our little pleasures in life.

Quinn served out his term as Chairman and was succeeded, much to most people's surprise, by another resident of

Shrewsbury Road and the man who followed in the footsteps of Peter Sutherland, the eminent barrister, Dermot Gleeson SC.

Gleeson had acted for AIB at the DIRT Inquiry. Tough and uncompromising, he had an excellent reputation in the Law Library where he was known as the highest-priced barrister in his field. But it is also said that if he thought a case was good enough, and more importantly the cause was good enough, he would waive his fee altogether.

Gleeson had been Attorney General in John Bruton's 'Rainbow' government in 1994 and following the 1997 General Election, when the three-way coalition of Fine Gael, Labour and the Democratic Left failed to win a majority, he went back to the Bar. He was the natural choice to act for AIB because of his legal reputation, but there was also the compromising connection to Lochlann Quinn through his brother Ruairi to take into consideration. Gleeson and Ruairi Quinn had served in Cabinet together.

In his closing submission he had told the members of the DIRT Inquiry: 'I don't envy you your task. I don't envy you – on top of an exhausting six weeks and reading of endless papers, burning of midnight oil and so on – the difficulties of assessing the issues, figuring out the precise remit of the Committee, the key issues on which you have to decide, and reaching conclusions.'

In the end his argument was not accepted, but witnesses from AIB who had seen him in action were obviously so impressed by his eloquence that they put him on the board of the company and, in a very short time, made him Chairman. In some ways he was the new, caring face of AIB.

Allied Irish Banks did not disappear completely from the limelight, but when the next crisis arose, as a result of overcharging for foreign exchange transactions, it was handled in a more transparent manner than previous indiscretions.

Life too has been good to Peter Sutherland who left AIB after sorting out the mess and sealing in the smell in 1993. He doesn't live on Shrewsbury Road, but he could afford to if he wanted. It's just that he prefers nearby Eglinton Road which does not attract as much attention as its close Ballsbridge neighbour.

By the time of the DIRT Inquiry, the former Fine Gael Attorney General had made as big a mark on the international stage as he did in the smaller environment of Irish business, politics and the law. He had gone on to negotiate the GATT Agreement and he had joined the boards of Goldman Sachs and BP. As the years went by, Peter Sutherland became an international institution. He was also independently wealthy after making over STG£100 million with the flotation of Goldman Sachs.

He would even go on to become known as 'God's Banker' but before that he would come to the attention of the interminable Moriarty Tribunal investigating Ansbacher accounts, Guinness & Mahon Bank and illicit payments to Charlie Haughey.

It was ironic to some observers that the two men could be mentioned in connection with the same dodgy offshore accounts, coming, as they did, from two very separate streams of Irish political life. Haughey was the street fighter who lined his pockets with the help of wealthy men and refused to pay his IR£250,000 'debt of honour' to AIB. Sutherland, on the other hand, was the Attorney General with long connections to Fine Gael and Garret FitzGerald, a man of probity and former Chairman of AIB.

But in the course of its exhaustive investigations, the Moriarty Tribunal discovered that Sutherland had, in June 1976, received 'bridging finance' from Guinness & Mahon Bank to buy an elegant house in Sydney Avenue, Blackrock, for £37,000. Maybe it wasn't odd for a busy and well-paid barrister but Sutherland, it appears, stayed on 'bridging finance' for almost ten years until the mid-1980s.

He was, at the time, he said, 'Less than attentive to my own financial affairs.'

Oddly enough, it also appeared from documentation that this loan was secured on a 'back to back' loan of £12,000 in an offshore account in the Channel Islands. Sutherland told the Moriarty Tribunal that he was unaware of any such account connected to his 'bridging finance'.

'He has informed the Tribunal that his father-in-law, a Spanish national and resident in Spain, had established a discretionary trust in the Channel Islands and that this had been established through Guinness & Mahon. Mr Sutherland has not been able to establish whether the account is one and the same as the account held in the discretionary trust. He has, however, provided the Tribunal with documentation from his Spanish relatives and from Spanish lawyers indicating how the trust in question was set up and how Irish tax advisors were involved in choosing the form of the trust and the location of the trust funds. It appears from documents made available from Mr Sutherland that these funds, originally settled in the Channel Islands, were ultimately resettled in January of 1980 in the Cayman Islands with Guinness Mahon Cayman Trust.'

Although such accounts in the name of Charles Haughey, for example, might warrant a great deal of suspicion, because of Sutherland's august position in Irish society and the international financial community, the Moriarty Tribunal fully accepted his explanation for the offshore account.

Since then, Sutherland has become a philanthropist and financial advisor to Pope Benedict XVI, which is how he earned the moniker 'God's Banker'.

His Chief Executive during those years at AIB, Gerald Scanlan, has also had the misfortune to become involved in the tangled world of offshore accounts, but luckily he was long gone from Allied Irish Banks when that surfaced. Like many other eminent figures, he seemed completely unaware of where a large amount of his money was held.

Following his retirement from AIB, Scanlan became a senior steward of the Turf Club, the body that runs Irish horse racing, and in the financial world he was appointed Chairman of the Irish Stock Exchange. Some observers found this quite ironic given that he still held this position when details of the infamous 'Dana Affair' surfaced for the first time in 1998.

But the feisty banker was in fine form during his appearances at the DIRT Inquiry. He seemed to regard the whole matter as an impertinence and gave the impression that during his time at Allied Irish Banks he had more to be doing than worrying about whether customers were opening offshore accounts or not.

His public pronouncements turned to embarrassment when, in May 2004, Allied Irish Banks revealed that Scanlan was one of four top executives of the bank who were beneficiaries of a company registered in the British Virgin Islands called Faldor. The company, the Irish Financial Services Regulatory Authority found, was the beneficiary of 'inappropriate favourable deal allocations by way of artificial deals' from AIB investment managers.

What exactly this means remains clouded in confusion, but it appears that the company got preferential deals on shares which were issued through the investment arm of the bank. In 2006, the four, including Scanlan, settled with the Revenue Commissioners for €323,313.

In a statement Scanlan said that he and his wife had invested funds with AIB investment managers in 1985 with the bank having 'sole and total investment discretion' of these funds. The sum had grown to £74,000 by 1989 when it was transferred to Faldor 'without our knowledge'. Like the 'Dana Affair', the mysterious 'Faldor' was never investigated by the Irish Stock Exchange and it too has disappeared into the cutting library where it remains largely forgotten.

Jim Culliton, another member of the board of AIB with a business and public service pedigree almost unrivalled in Ireland, became another casualty of the Ansbacher offshore account scandal in the middle of the DIRT hearings.

Culliton, the former Chairman of building company CRH, was Chairman of AIB in the time between Sutherland's departure and the arrival of Lochlann Quinn. As Chairman of the Audit

Committee, he was the man charged with investigating Anthony Spollen's allegations in 1991. He had also been Chairman of the RTÉ Authority and had been appointed by the Irish government that same year to assemble the 'Culliton Report' which became the blueprint for Irish economic strategy around the mid-1990s, pulling the country from a 'basket case' economy to being one of the richest nations in the world.

When it was revealed in late September 1990 that he was an account holder with Ansbacher Cayman Bank, the offshore bank run by his colleague in CRH Des Traynor, Culliton resigned from all his directorships citing 'personal reasons'.

Although he had to suffer the ignominy of being chased down Kildare Street from the DIRT hearings by Charlie Bird and a posse of reporters, the Chairman of the Inquiry, Jim Mitchell, regarded Culliton as the most truthful witness to appear at the hearings. Whether that is any consolation to Culliton, who has since disappeared from public life, is another matter.

Although he derived no satisfaction from the tribulation of Allied Irish Banks and its various executives, Anthony Spollen did have the satisfaction of having his position vindicated ten years after leaving the bank in July 1991.

Having lost the boardroom struggle, he had little choice but to go at the time. But he went with a 'golden handshake' estimated at almost IR£500,000 and a five-year contract as an 'international' consultant for the bank. By the time of the DIRT hearings he was 'a pensioner' of the bank.

Spollen became a close advisor to hotelier Paddy Fitzpatrick and a director of his hotel chain. He also wrote *Corporate Fraud,* an illuminating account of the dire consequences of what happens when a company is not properly controlled. In 2006, he became a director of the newly privatised Aer Lingus, proving that there are those who still value his skills as a financial analyst and a man of international business experience.

For most of those involved in the tumultuous times of the early 1990s, life moved on. Tony 'The Boot' McCarthy and most others in the higher echelons of the Revenue Commissioners have retired to enjoy their golf or the GAA. The DIRT Inquiry, momentous as it was at the time, has largely faded from the public memory.

One man, however, is still stuck with his memories. Jimmy Livingstone, the tax inspector who organised the raids on the tax dodgers in Milltown Malbay in Co Clare and discovered that small town Ireland was saturated with bogus non-resident accounts, still lives with the bloody murder of his wife, Grace. Nobody was ever charged and the mystery surrounding her death remains. People believe what they believe and, in some ways, Livingstone has come to accept that too.

He thinks he may know the answer but, as of yet, he hasn't decided to tell anyone. Sometimes, late at night, over a glass of whiskey, he'll talk with a visitor about those days when almost nobody knew his name and the banks were running rings around the tax authorities. And a little bitterness will creep into the conversation as he speaks about the banks and their revenge. But maybe he takes it all too personally. Maybe it was just business.

And if it was illegal, who was to know? And when it did become known, those who knew were paid off, or pensioned off, or disappeared off.

Others who knew didn't do anything because they concerned themselves with great affairs of State. They didn't want to disturb the 'little people' with the unsavoury details.

And, only for a real whistleblower, nobody would have ever known.

Irish Family Feuds

Battles over Money, Sex and Power

LIAM COLLINS

When families fall out, the bitterness that emerges is matched only by the ferocity of their attacks on each other. Family feuds are far more vicious than disputes between strangers, as family members compete to crush each other completely and without mercy.

Cases include many rich and famous Irish families:

- Ben v Margaret – Duel at Dunnes
- The PV Doyle family 'hotel' war
- Comans and the 'Pub brawl'
- Enya, Clannad and the Brennan family feud
- 'Volkswagon vendetta' – the O'Flahertys' family secret

and many more family feuds over money, power and sex.

Irish Crimes of Passion

Killing for Love, Lust and Desire

LIAM COLLINS

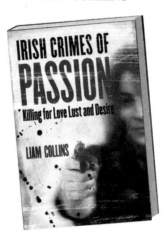

Liam Collins investigates the tragic cases where love, lust, desire and jealousy twist and contort in a spiral of madness.

- Picture the beautiful temptress who buys her own grave, then lures her lover to a dramatic death scene in her bedroom . . .
- the husband who goes through his wife's mobile phone messages and unleashes a rage that not only leads to her murder but wipes out an entire family . . .
- or the coward brooding in a love triangle who hires a ruthless killer to murder his pregnant wife.

The are all here in the hidden Ireland, where ordinary men and women suddenly get caught up in that deadly moment when crime and passion collide.